Crime in the city: Kilkenny in 1845

Maynooth Studies in Local History

SERIES EDITOR Raymond Gillespie

This volume is one of six short books published in the Maynooth Studies in Local History series in 2015. Like their predecessors they range widely, both chronologically and geographically, over the local experience in the Irish past. Chronologically they span the world of customary law in medieval Gowran to Nenagh and Galway in the early twentieth century. Geographically they range across the country from Callan to Gowran and Kilkenny, through the midlands at Nenagh to east Galway and north to Dublin. Socially they move from the landed worlds of Revd Thomas Goff or the Burkes of Ballydugan to the middle class of Callan and the medieval burghers of Gowran, through the revolutionary generation of Nenagh to the criminal world of Kilkenny city. In doing so they demonstrate the vitality of the study of local history in Ireland and reveal the range of possibilities open to anyone interested in studying the local past. Those possibilities involve the dissection of the local experience in the complex and contested social worlds of which it is part as people strove to preserve and enhance their positions within their local societies. Such studies of local worlds over such long periods are vital for the future since they not only stretch the historical imagination but provide a longer perspective on the evolution of local societies in Ireland and help us to understand more fully the complex evolution of the Irish experience. These works do not simply chronicle events relating to an area within administrative or geographically-determined boundaries, but open the possibility of understanding how and why particular regions had their own personality in the past. Such an exercise is clearly one of the most exciting challenges for the future.

Like their predecessors these six short books are reconstructions of the socially diverse worlds of the poor as well as the rich, women as well as men, and reconstruct the way in which those who inhabited those worlds lived their daily lives, often little affected by the large themes that dominate the writing of national history. In addressing these issues, studies such as those presented in these short books, together with their predecessors, are at the forefront of Irish historical research and represent some of the most innovative and exciting work being undertaken in Irish history today. They also provide models that others can follow up and adapt in their own studies of the Irish past. In such ways will we understand better the regional diversity of Ireland and the social and cultural basis for that diversity. They, with their predecessors, convey the vibrancy and excitement of the world of Irish local history today.

Maynooth Studies in Local History: Number 121

Crime in the city
Kilkenny in 1845

Fergal Donoghue

FOUR COURTS PRESS

Set in 10pt on 12pt Bembo by
Carrigboy Typesetting Services for
FOUR COURTS PRESS LTD
7 Malpas Street, Dublin 8, Ireland
www.fourcourtspress.ie
and in North America for
FOUR COURTS PRESS
c/o ISBS, 920 N.E. 58th Avenue, Suite 300, Portland, OR 97213

ISBN 978–1–84682–581–1

Printed in Ireland
by SPRINT-Print, Dublin.

Introduction

During 1845, Kilkenny City was on the brink of dramatic social and economic changes, not least those initiated by the Famine that first appeared in that year. While studies have been done on rural society in pre-Famine Ireland, little has been written on the urban world in the same period. A study of crime and sentencing, and an examination of general social and living conditions within the city of Kilkenny in 1845 allows an insight into the wider questions of life in the city immediately prior to the Famine and provides a counterbalance to the rural bias of writing about this period. By looking at a single year in an urban setting on the brink of the great Famine, it is hoped to illustrate how society was structured and how it functioned. The manner in which it dealt with civil disobedience offers a particular perspective for this snapshot of the city at a particular point in time.

Crime and sentencing is an issue that has received very little attention in a local historical context for a variety of reasons.[1] The loss of documentary sources is one reason. On a national level there are relatively few extant records to do with local crime and disorder. Files from the quarter sessions often made their way into the possession of the crown solicitors on circuit and were retained locally in private hands and often lost. There are fragmentary survivals from this period; a petty sessions book for Westport for 1831, for example, survives in the National Library of Ireland.[2] The administration of the petty sessions changed with the Petty Sessions (Ireland) Act of 1851 and as a result most of the petty sessions records only survive from this period onwards. For the city of Kilkenny in 1845 there are no surviving sessions books and just one original court record was found – a summary of the assizes for the county for spring 1845 written by the crown solicitor for the southern circuit, William Kemmis.[3] There are particular difficulties in using other sources, such as the records of the Chief Secretary's Office, to fill the gaps. The fact that they are written from the point of view of the authorities is one problem. However, sources such as the convict reference files provide a different perspective and, uniquely, detail events from the point of view of the convicted prisoner in the form of a petition.

While at first glance there seems to be a dearth of primary sources for this subject, in fact a wealth of information is available. Parliamentary papers, for example, contain statistics relating to crime and sentencing, gaol conditions, the conditions of the labouring classes and census information, among other topics. The local newspapers detail the court cases and the trials, including the city quarter sessions and city petty sessions. They also report on more local courts, such as those held in the borough of Irishtown that dealt with simple matters mostly to do with debts and cases of *distringas,* a process of recovering debts not exceeding 40s. The newspapers also contain information on general social and living conditions at the time, while the extant board of guardians' minute books detail social conditions in the poor law union of Kilkenny. Their fortnightly meetings were also summarized in the local newspapers and such summaries act as substitutes for years for which the minute books are missing. The Kilkenny Corporation minute books mostly deal with the day-to-day running and the finances of the city, but a number of letters and comments within them also discuss the social conditions at the time.

The year 1845 was chosen as the focus of this short book because of the availability of certain sources, such as the census of 1841.[4] This is widely regarded as the first accurate Irish census and provides a wealth of information. Aside from its obvious use in determining population levels, it has a detailed breakdown of employment in the city at the time allowing patterns in employment to be determined. Were there districts in which particular types of employment were concentrated, for example? The census also has a classification of housing types that can be used to examine the numbers and types of housing. An analysis of the census can therefore reveal much about the inhabitants of the city in the early 1840s, detailing employment, types of employment and in some respects housing conditions. It also casts light on the relationship between population density and employment. How these factors are reflected in levels of crime is one of the key questions that this work seeks to answer.

There are other sources that will supplement the census in describing life in the city immediately prior to 1845, by providing evidence of general social and living conditions. The Poor Law Inquiry took place between 1833 and 1836. It was set up by royal commission to inquire into the conditions of the poorer classes in Ireland and to determine what steps were necessary to alleviate poverty.[5] Through the testimonies of the witnesses it called and the information it collected this inquiry is a detailed investigation of social conditions and attitudes in Ireland a decade before the Famine. For instance, it covers deserted and orphan children, illegitimate children, widows with children, those who were impotent through age, the sick poor, the able bodied out of work. It also deals with vagrancy, destitution, labourers' earnings, cottier tenants, food, drinking and emigration.[6] Since much of this evidence was collected from local witnesses it is an important window into the conditions of the local Kilkenny community in 1845.

Crime is, after all, concerned with individuals in a community, so an examination of the community may suggest or reveal motivations for crime and civil unrest. It may also illustrate reasons behind specific types of crime. Was a lack of food reflected in the theft of same? Are circumstances of vagrancy and destitution to be found in the evidence presented by those committed for their crimes? These are questions and themes that were also raised in the evidence taken before the Devon Commission of 1845 in which the principal evidence for Kilkenny city came from Barnaby Scott, a solicitor, and the mayor of Kilkenny at the time, Edmond Smithwick.[7] While this evidence is mainly about the conditions of the occupation of land in Ireland it also dealt with local Kilkenny matters such as evictions, the average rate of pay for labourers in the city, leases, farm improvements and the condition of the labouring classes. The evidence of the mayor is of particular significance as he was well informed about the social conditions of the city, albeit from a particular perspective.[8] Also of use, in both determining social conditions and providing a general background to crime, is a parliamentary paper concerning the state of Ireland in respect of crime.[9] This paper, which was published in 1839, provides context for crime in the years prior to the Famine. It is particularly useful in describing the structure of the judicial system at the time. The evidence given by several crown solicitors described how juries were selected for petty and quarter sessions as well as discussing court procedure. For Kilkenny city one of the respondents was a magistrate, Robert Greene.[10] His evidence was concerned with law and order (or indeed disorder) in Kilkenny and touched on the duties of juries, the quarter sessions, Ribbonism, assistance from the central administration and the Chief Secretary's Office at the time. It detailed how he corresponded with the Chief Secretary's Office and the manner in which questions were answered. General conduct at election times was discussed as was the general state of the county. Also of value is the evidence given by the crown solicitor for the Leinster circuit, William Kemmis.[11] His evidence provides an overview of the duties of the crown solicitors at the time, allowing an insight into the structure of the legal system. He also discussed the general nature of social order in the county. His replies to the commissioners, while often impressionistic, are particularly valuable on the perceptions of crime among contemporaries. For instance, when questioned on whether the county was more or less tranquil than it was five years previous he replied that it was 'more so'.[12] Further evidence from respondents to this inquiry reveal details on jury selection in terms of the relevant qualification to sit on a jury and how the juries bill affected an improvement on juries picked for quarter sessions.[13] The Chief Secretary's Office Registered Papers for Kilkenny also contain references to both the city gaol and the courts. There are very few surviving records of the courts themselves, but in papers belonging to the crown solicitor for the Leinster circuit, William Kemmis, there survives the return of cases for trial for the Spring assizes of 1845.[14]

The information contained in these parliamentary papers is complemented by the local sources, mainly on the condition of the inhabitants of the city. These include the corporation minute books and the extant board of guardians' minute books as well as the two local newspapers, the *Kilkenny Moderator* and the *Kilkenny Journal*. While the corporation minute books are primarily concerned with the week-to-week expenditure of the corporation they also include transcripts of several letters that give some detail on general conditions at the time.[15] For example, a letter written by the corporation to parliament concerning the repeal of the Union in the 1840s reveals an awareness of the levels of unemployment at the time: 'Representatives of a City which once bid fair to be the leading manufacturing District of Ireland but whose poverty and distress consequent upon want of employment now prevails and has prevailed for many years'.[16] A further letter discussed the need to write to the lord lieutenant asking that the expense of the constabulary be transferred to central government.[17] It seems that contemporaries thought that the cost of maintaining the constabulary was high despite its benefits in maintaining law and order. The board of guardians' minute books also provide important material on the state of the city for the study period.[18] As early as January 1845, for instance, inmates of the workhouse were requesting assistance in emigrating, suggesting that conditions were already deteriorating locally.[19] They also reveal an awareness of the seasonal level of unemployment at the time. This is clear from several references detailing attempts to set up an allotment system to 'enable agricultural labourers to support their families in seasons of deficient employment'.[20] The board of guardians' minute books also reveal the structural nature of unemployment and its consequences by ascribing unemployment to the 'inability of the occupying tenantry to hire a sufficient number of workmen for the proper cultivation of their farms'. The consequence of this was that the labourers had no work and were therefore not paid and thus unable to obtain 'the necessary quantity of ground for cultivating an annual crop of potatoes'.[21]

In determining the levels of detected crime brought to trial one of the more useful sources is the parliamentary return of committals in Ireland.[22] Considering the lack of extant gaol and court records the returns of committals allows for an examination of the extent of detected crime. They are broken down into the numbers committed, indicted and convicted and are of most use when supplemented with the information from the local newspapers because more detail on the relevant petty sessions, quarter sessions and assizes and particulars of the cases are contained in these. Detail on the actual court sessions comes from the local newspapers, the *Kilkenny Moderator* and the *Kilkenny Journal*: they describe the proceedings on the day of the trial, list the juries and outline the cases before the court, often giving the testimony of the accused and some details of the judge's verdict.

Linked to the problem of crime is the question of punishment. One of the most common forms of punishment in Kilkenny was imprisonment in the city gaol. Parliamentary papers form the bulk of primary evidence concerning the administration of, and conditions within, the city gaol because gaol registers are not extant for the city gaol until 1898. Those individuals who were given a sentence of imprisonment were committed to the city gaol, which was located directly below the courthouse. A series of parliamentary papers describe the gaol conditions, its governance, staffing levels and general conditions. It was small, cramped and understaffed and year after year received less than favourable reports as to its general conditions. Most of the information on the Kilkenny city gaol comes from the annual reports on the prisons of Ireland.[23] These reports state that it contained 16 cells, 5 day rooms, 3 yards, an infirmary and a kitchen. There are, however, discrepancies in the reports describing the number of rooms in the prison. The precise reason for this discrepancy is unclear.[24] Conditions were very poor, and most of the cells were below ground level and thus poorly lit and ventilated. Prisoners were also not properly separated into groups of those that were convicted and those on remand. The only employment was breaking rocks for gravel for the repair of roads and footpaths. There was no prison clothing, neither was there a school, as was common in other prisons. The female prisoners were occasionally put to work washing clothes or doing needle work. The food was noted to be of 'good quality' and report of 1842 states that the cost of feeding the prisoners was approximately 5d. per head per day.[25] Living conditions, therefore, were quite poor, which raises the question as to whether or not people were aware of them when committing offences and if in some cases being sentenced to gaol was actually seen as a severe enough punishment. Given how severely repeat offenders were treated, multiple offences were to be avoided, but was a short sentence of imprisonment sufficient deterrent for the general population?

The most obvious problem when dealing with the issue of crime and sentencing in Ireland is that the sources invariably come from the authorities and rarely from the point of view of the accused. One source that provides a rather different perspective are prisoners' memorials. These were letters written by prisoners (perhaps with some professional assistance) to the lord lieutenant in the hope that clemency would be granted and that the sentence would be commuted or indeed overturned.[26] Several of these exist for Kilkenny city for 1845. Some of these letters make up part of the files of the Chief Secretary's Office Registered Papers. In some instances only the letter acknowledging the pardon survives, in other instances the memorials consist of a lengthy letter to the lord lieutenant presenting the case for clemency.[27] Taken together this evidence provides the basis for the reconstruction of the legal system in Kilkenny on the eve of the Famine and in doing so casts considerable light on crime in the city. The evidence is not unproblematic but it does reveal much about the urban courts in 1845 and opens a window into the world of pre-Famine Kilkenny.

1. Kilkenny in 1845

In 1845, the city of Kilkenny consisted of approximately 921 acres and comprised part of the parishes of St Patrick, St Canice, St Mary, St Maul and St John.[1] Until the boundary revisions of the early 1840s, the city had consisted of the entirety of these parishes and together they formed the County of the City of Kilkenny (fig. 1).[2]

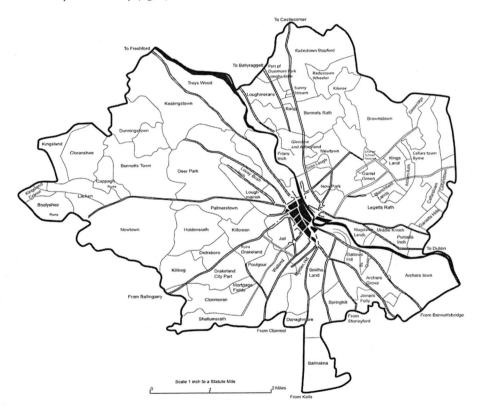

1. County of the City of Kilkenny re-drawn from the municipal corporations report of 1837.

The new, smaller, area of the town was established by the Municipal Corporations Act of 1840 (fig. 2). By 1844 the land outside the new smaller municipal boundary,

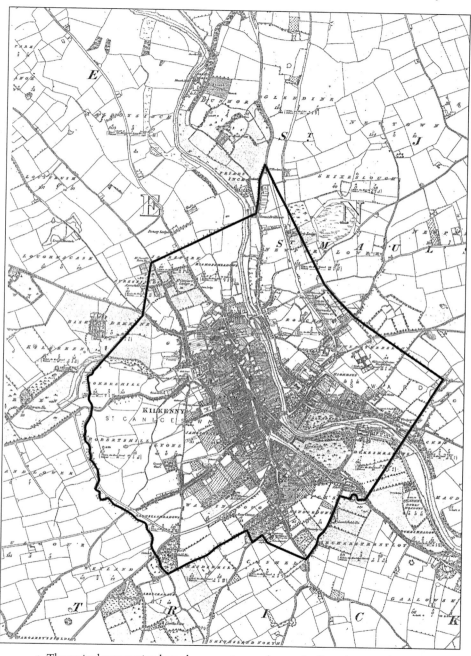

2. The revised corporation boundary superimposed on to the first edition Ordnance Survey map of 1840, reproduced under permit number MP 000415.

but within the older boundary, became a barony in itself, the barony of Kilkenny, which was deemed to be part of the county at large.

Responsibility for administering justice within this larger area of the barony of Kilkenny ultimately passed to the county courts but that was not a predetermined or obvious development.[3] In the years after 1840 there was some jurisdictional confusion and it was not clear whether the city courts or county courts had jurisdiction over the barony of Kilkenny. However, in late 1844 or early 1845 the area within the reformed municipal boundary of 1840 had effectively become the re-defined County of the City of Kilkenny and thus delimits the area covered by this book.

The main street of the city itself lies along a north-south axis with side streets radiating off this axis. The river Nore flows through the city and is crossed by John's Bridge and Green's Bridge. There are high points of land at either end of the city. Kilkenny castle occupies the northern one with St Canice's cathedral on the elevated site to the south. In 1845 the city lay between these two sites. The population of the city at this time was roughly 19,066.[4] It was a predominantly urban world but with a considerable agricultural hinterland for which the city was the most important marketing centre. No town or city exists in isolation. What were perceived as local events often had their genesis in wider world and national developments that had powerful local impacts. By 1845 Ireland's economy was largely export based. In the early 19th century trade had grown on the back of a dramatically improved road network, and the advent of steamships for shorter journeys made crossing the Irish sea in particular significantly cheaper. Goods from rural communities were sold at urban markets in the principal towns and villages and transported from there to ports. The export market was mostly in cattle and grain, both of which were in large demand in a rapidly industrializing England. Cattle exports tripled in the period from 1830 to 1845 to meet the demand for meat from industrial cities in England as that country became increasingly wealthy.[5]

There was also, and most significantly, a massive increase in the Irish population, which put significant strain on the resources of Ireland and created social tensions that manifested themselves in outbreaks of rural disorder. Although population growth had slowed by 1845 the huge increase in population had a knock-on effect on living standards that were in steady decline. This decline in living standards was most obvious at the margins of society where many relied on the potato and on the practice of conacre. Conacre was a system of letting small amounts of land, usually on an 11-month basis, for growing crops, mostly the potato; it gave few legal rights to the tenant and rent was paid in cash or labour.[6] Even in an urban setting like Kilkenny city the practice of conacre had an impact. While most of the city's population relied on buying and selling goods at markets to make a living, many of the urban poorer classes were reliant on conacre for their livelihood and dependant on the potato crop for their main source of nutrition. Even after the changes to the city boundaries in the various Municipal Corporations Acts, Kilkenny city still had an extensive agricultural hinterland and it is likely that the practices outlined above were prevalent in these areas. Evidence from the poor law reports seems to support this.[7] The board of guardians of Kilkenny union were acutely aware of the problems that the practice of conacre produced and of the levels of unemployment associated with small holdings of limited tenurial duration. This is clear from several references detailing attempts to set up an allotment system in the city in 1845 in an effort to 'enable agricultural labourers to support their families in seasons of deficient employment'.[8] An entry in the minute book states 'that land allotments connected with accommodation from Loan Funds are eminently calculated to enable agricultural labourers to support their families in seasons of deficient employment'.[9] When discussing rates it was noted 'that such a destitution of agricultural labourers is occasioned by want of employment and other means of supplying themselves by their own industry with a stock of provisions'.[10] The debate concerning allotments continued throughout the year but was eventually abandoned when it was put to a vote to petition parliament for permission to proceed with it.[11]

The problems of both urban and rural poverty come into clearest focus through the local workings of the poor law. Following the findings of the poor law enquiry of the early 1830s, a poor law for Ireland was finally implemented in 1838, although this was very different from that suggested by the findings of the poor law reports, being mostly based on the English system. The poor law was workhouse based, offering indoor relief for the poor in Ireland, with an estimated 80,000 beds made available in the first phase of workhouses, most of which were built by 1845. The workhouse in Kilkenny could hold 1,300 inmates. On 4 January 1845, 754 people were resident.[12] The number of inmates in the workhouse remained close to this level for the rest of the year. A combination of high population levels and rising poverty, as evidenced by the work of the poor law, was reflected in rising emigration levels. Another solution to the problem of increasing poverty in the region was assisted emigration from the workhouse in Kilkenny city and there are several references to the desirability of some sort of assisted emigration scheme from the Kilkenny workhouse starting in early 1845 when 'Mr James moved that application having been made by some inmates of this house to be assisted to emigrate'. References to assisted emigration continued throughout the minute book for the rest of the year.[13] How these levels of unemployment, want of food, and general poverty shaped the world of Kilkenny on the eve of the Famine is the focus of the remainder of this chapter. One of the best ways of exploring that is through the 1841 census and this can be supplemented by the work of Dr Robert Cane, a physician to the workhouse and fever hospital. His important 1849 pamphlet, *Some practical remarks on cholera with an appendix containing sanatory hints for Kilkenny*, comments extensively on housing conditions and overcrowding in the city during the cholera epidemics of the early 1830s and he also comments on the general state of the city in the late 1840s.[14]

KILKENNY CITY IN THE CENSUS OF 1841

The first accurate census of Kilkenny took place as part of the national census of 1841. This provides a snapshot of life in the city on the eve of the Famine (table 1). In terms of the total population of Kilkenny city 46 per cent were male and 54 per cent were female and the age structure of the population was heavily weighted between the ages of 16 and 45 with a peak in the 16–25 years cohort.

Table 1. Population of Kilkenny city in 1841 by age groups as outlined in the census [15]

Age Groups	Male	Female	Total	Percentage
0–5 years	1,257	1,299	2,556	13.41
6–15	1,936	1,867	3,803	19.95
16–25	1,789	2,286	4,075	21.37
26–35	1,360	1,624	2,984	15.65
36–45	980	1,292	2,272	11.92
46–55	758	987	1,745	9.15
56–65	466	613	1,079	5.66
66–75	164	216	380	1.99
76–85	45	91	136	0.71
86–100	8	28	36	0.19
Totals	**8,763**	**10,303**	**19,066**	**100**
	46%	54 %		

This data provides not only an overview of the urban population of Kilkenny but also allows an insight into the sort of problems associated with living in the city. Given the problem of poverty, linked to unemployment and underemployment as discussed above, the census data allows a rudimentary assessment of employment levels. This can be arrived at by making some assumptions about the proportion of the population available for work based on the age structure recorded in the census. If the under 15 age group, which made up just over 33 per cent of the population, are excluded, the majority of the adult population belonged to the 16–55 age group. This grouping of 11,056 individuals made up approximately 58 per cent of the overall population. In conjunction with other elements of the census and using the hypothesis that the majority of the working population was in the 16–55 age group this suggests that the remaining 42 per cent were dependant on the working population, which is a high rate of dependency given the problems of unemployment and underemployment that existed, and produced a very vulnerable population. This is clearly a very basic assessment. Furthermore, it can not take into account errors in the census or if information was deliberately misrepresented to the census enumerators. However, the problem was more acute than this suggests.

Table 2 shows the structure of the working population using the employment classifications employed in the census. Here the employment figure is given as 7,205 (or 6,993 of those over 15) with the remaining 3,851 (or over a third of the labour force) unemployed. In 1849 Dr Cane commented that '6,062 human beings or nearly one third of the whole had no specified occupation'.[16] The 1841 census also records a very high proportion of those employed as being 'unclassified' which may suggest general labourers who were particularly vulnerable to changes in employment levels as a result of even minor economic variations. The data certainly suggests chronic underemployment, and in some circumstances unemployment, but it is clear that a substantial proportion of the population lived a perilous existence on edge of subsistence. High levels of unemployment are also evidenced in the report on the sanitary conditions of the city published in 1849.[17]

Table 2. Breakdown of occupations and employment by employment type and gender in Kilkenny city based on the 1841 census

Kilkenny city census 1841				
Employment summary				
	Over 15 years		Under 15 years	
Occupations	Males	Females	Males	Females
Ministering to food	805	156	35	12
Ministering to clothing	1,056	674	34	21
Ministering to lodging, furniture, machinery etc.	894	14	12	1
Ministering to health	27	12		
Ministering to charity	1	6		
Ministering to justice	103	1		
Ministering to education	38	22		
Ministering to religion	32	14		
Unclassified	1,811	1,327	20	77
Subtotals	4,767	2,226	101	111
Total in employment	7,205			
Total population	19,066			

The detail of the employment structure in table 2 reveals that men were the main breadwinners outside the home since employment opportunities leaned heavily towards the male population, while women were primarily engaged in working at home or in the sort of informal and erratic employment that was not recorded in formal census returns. This made them uniquely vulnerable if families broke up or the economy entered a downturn. There are numerous references in both the local newspapers and the board of guardians' records to mothers with children being abandoned by their partners or being refused entry to the workhouse because they were not a complete family. Such contexts may well be reasons for engaging in petty crime or resorting to petty larceny simply to survive.

As well as allowing a breakdown of the population, the census also permits an analysis of the various housing types in the city. Such an analysis is important since housing types are good indicators of levels of wealth. There were four main housing types based on valuation. Fourth-class houses were basically mud cabins with one room, third-class houses were considered of a better class but still built of mud and consisting of two-to-four rooms with windows, second-class houses were, in towns at least, a house in a street with five to nine rooms and windows, with first-class houses being 'all houses of a better description than the preceding classes'.[18] Some 62 per cent of the houses in Kilkenny city were mud cabins of the third or fourth class, suggesting a very substantial under class of the poor in the city. 31 per cent of the housing was second class with just 8 per cent being first class (table 3).

The location of these houses is also important. An examination of the houses based on the census, Griffith's valuation of the 1850s and the first edition Ordnance Survey map of the 1830s shows that the vast majority of the first-class houses lined the main streets of the town, High Street and Parliament Street, with the second-class houses located on the streets radiating off them. The third- and fourth-class houses were also located along these side streets as well as in the borough of Irishtown, beside St Canice's cathedral, and on the outskirts of the city. These third- and fourth-class houses on the outskirts of the city or on the side streets off the main streets were densely packed, and provided very poor living conditions. The lanes off High Street and the working-class cabins were described in 1832–4 as having 'filth, poverty, defective ventilation and sewerage as well as overcrowding of inhabitants in these plague spots'. In 1849 Dr Cane further described the cramped conditions of the lanes off High Street: 'the limited space occupied by Guard, Poyntz's, Collier's, and Chapel Lanes, lanes so dovetailed into each other as to be a neighbourhood in itself, and occupying a space, which, under a proper state of city building, would be but large enough for one of these lanes and its inhabitants'.[19]

Table 3. Classification of houses with numbers of families living in them based on the census of 1841

Class of houses	Houses	Percentage of house types one to four	Families	Percentage of families living in type one to four housing
1st	248	8	346	8.96
2nd	940	31	1,376	35.64
3rd	1,179	39	1,411	36.54
4th	690	23	728	18.86
Totals	**3,057**	**100**	**3,861**	**100**

With a housing stock of 3,057 and a population of 19,066 each house contained on average over 6.2 persons, suggesting a large household size. It is possible that in the case of first-class housing this was as a result of servants living in the house. In other cases, however, there were clearly multiple families living in each of the houses. This seems clear from the census recording of 3,057 houses but 3,861 families. Regarding the type 2 houses, multiple families in these houses appears to have been quite common with 1.4 families on average per house. With five to nine rooms in these houses living conditions, where multiple families were sharing the house, would have been cramped by modern standards but were probably manageable. The same cannot be said for types three and four houses which made up 62 per cent of houses, occupied by 56 per cent of the families in the city. These houses, made of mud with one to four rooms, would not have provided hygienic or comfortable living conditions. Space would have been at a premium and if pigs were kept inside, as was quite common in this class of house in other parts of Ireland, then this would have further lowered the standard of living.[20] Cane comments extensively on the condition of the poorer houses and the sanitary state of the inhabitants. His analysis demonstrates clearly that living conditions were cramped and standards of hygiene were poor. In describing the houses off High Street he comments that 'in the lanes many of the houses consist of a passage and eight rooms four above and four below; occasionally a family will be found in each of these rooms, where overcrowding and poverty and the habits it begets, and want of mean'.[21]

An analysis of the census indicates that a slight majority of families, some 2,139, were living in the lowest classes of housing. This is compared with the 1,722 living in the first- and second-class houses. Were poverty and deprivation significant factors in social unrest or in criminal behaviour? The census indicates high levels of unemployment and shows a higher percentage of the population living in the lowest classes of housing. This is also supported by the work of Dr Cane in his commentary. The question that must now be answered is how is this statistical analysis reflected in the actual living conditions at the time? Is the information from the census reflected in alternative sources and if so are the living conditions a reason for particular kinds of crime?

SOCIAL AND LIVING CONDITIONS

By the 19th century the parishes of St Canice and St Maul were the poorer parts of the city. These are the parishes that lie outside the high status core of Hightown. The parish of St Canice occupied most of Irishtown and the streets around it. The parish of St Maul was the smallest and most underdeveloped and it lay entirely outside the city walls. Neither parish developed to the same extent as those of St John and St Mary where the majority of the commercial, local government and manufacturing buildings were located. By the late 1830s, according to the poor enquiry, the parishes of St Canice and St Maul contained approximately 200 widows and 600 children with no visible means of support while just under 300 people subsisted by begging. These figures do not, however, tally with the recorded number of paupers in the census of 1841, which noted only 41 paupers. Either the census enumerators were incorrect or the respondents to the poor law enquiry were exaggerating the numbers. Given the problems of identifying and counting a shifting population on the edge of subsistence the former explanation is more likely to be correct. There were no recorded instances of anyone having died from destitution in the parishes of the city although it was acknowledged by the vicar of St Mary's in 1835 that 'I fear there have been cases in which the existence of the aged poor has been shortened by great privations'.[22] In relation to poverty and social conditions the poor law report shows that there were low levels of child desertion in the city.[23]

This pattern of poverty was replicated, though to a lesser extent, in many of the other parishes of the city. All the existing evidence of the parliamentary papers on employment, wages, diet, housing conditions, land rental, conacre and emigration suggests that most parishes had a substantial body of the poor within their bounds who were either unemployed or underemployed. The poor law reports reveal that the population was seen to be 'little better than starving' when out of work, with a diet consisting of 'potatoes with sour milk, or a salt herring occasionally; their clothing of the worst description'. Wages were relatively low with a daily rate being between 1s. in the summer and 8d. in the winter without diet and 10d. in the summer and 6d. in the winter with food provided. The average yearly wage for a labourer without diet was about £8 with the average yearly expense for food being also £8 or 'if properly fed, it would be £12'.[24] The market costs for food would have placed purchasing provisions as a way of obtaining a healthier diet beyond the means of low wage earners. Flour, for example, was 16s.–28s. a bag, with pigs being sold for an average of 38s.[25] Rent was also quite high, from £3–£4 if the house had land and from £1–£2 otherwise. The lowest class of accommodation, the types three and four houses, were described as 'in general wretched hovels'.[26] The poor living conditions were in part attributed to the downturn in the woollen trade: 'the general condition of the poor is very much deteriorated since 1815 in consequence of the woollen trade which was then in a very flourishing state, being now almost extinct'.[27] The Devon Commission report of 1845 also provided evidence of high unemployment and poor living conditions within Kilkenny city. It adds further information on market costs and the costs of exporting goods as opposed to selling them locally. The respondent for the city of Kilkenny was the mayor, Edmond Smithwick. He stated that the export of grain and other farm produce was barely, if at all, profitable, and that the lack of employment led to there being no market for goods locally. The general population were simply not able to afford to buy goods at market prices.[28] A letter to the *Kilkenny Moderator* published in the edition of 28 May 1845 suggests that goods bought at cost often had a mark-up of 40–50 per cent: this was solely to the benefit of the traders and not to that of either the farmer or the lower classes, 'in many cases the forestallers purchased from the farmer at first cost. He then sells to huxters or small dealers of course at a profit. The huxters then retail to the poor and of course at a profit'.[29] The author of this letter, William Wilson, had the intention of buying potatoes at cost and selling them on at the same cost to the poor. While farming and the livelihoods of middle-class farmers seemed to be improving there was 'a vast want of employment' among the labouring classes, while labourers could be hired for as little as 4*d*. a day with food 'which diet is any thing but nutriment'.[30] Market prices for goods were still quite high in 1845 and on a level with the prices from the mid-1830s while the cost of buying goods at market was still outside the reach of the labouring classes. Rentals for the labouring classes in towns and villages were approximately 40*s*. per year with the average wage still being 8*d*. per day. Rent, therefore, was still between £1 and £2 annually for the labouring classes. The practice of conacre was still prevalent with the cost of renting the land being £8–£10 per acre. The problems highlighted in the poor enquiry were still there, with the labouring classes said to be 'a great portion of the year without employment'.[31] The Devon Commission report was extensively commented on in the *Kilkenny Moderator* shortly after its publication.[32]

Further support for this picture painted by the governmental enquirers is provided by the commentary of Dr Cane. He described the area around the Black Abbey and Blackmill Street in the parish of St Canice as being 'then much more crowded than it now is'. He further described the houses around Greenshill and Broguemakers Hill, which lie in both St Maul's and St Canice's parishes, as being 'densely crowded, and of the most miserable description, filled to overflowing with potato beggars and a class of wretched cottiers'.[33] These sort of social conditions with high levels of unemployment coupled with large amounts of begging, a poor diet and inadequate clothing may have been a factor in the larceny of foodstuffs and garments. An analysis of the cases of larceny particularly at the petty sessions, discussed in the final chapter of this short book, supports this hypothesis.

With poverty and unemployment still at such high levels in the 1840s the question must be asked if the distress this poverty created might have fed into the pattern of crime in Kilkenny. Were the labouring classes, who would have been most seriously affected by this deprivation, primarily those who appeared in the court system as a result? Despite this evidence for extensive poverty in the city many contemporaries did not equate it with the levels of crime. Local newspapers, for instance, did not equate the deteriorating social conditions with the incidence of crime in the city and the surrounding countryside on the eve of the Famine. Numerous editorials, particularly in the *Kilkenny Moderator*, described conditions throughout the year. An editorial of 5 July 1845, for example, states that 'this County is at present in a state of perfect tranquillity'.[34] Addresses made by the county and city barrister to juries at quarter sessions were frequently reported in the newspapers and generally these comments suggest that the county and the city were quite peaceable at the time. A quotation from the January quarter sessions in 1845 illuminates this point: 'The Barrister then said that he had just before, in charging the County Grand Jury, expressed great pleasure at the lightness of the business in the county, and he had now much more pleasure in congratulating them on the peaceful state of their city'.[35] Comments of this sort were typical of the remaining sittings of the quarter sessions for the year. Much of the local evidence also seems to suggest that the levels of crime were low and the city was in a relatively peaceable condition in the early 1840s. Clearly, the evidence of the newspaper reports, suggesting a docile city, contrasts strongly with the evidence of the parliamentary papers and other sources that suggest a city that was occupied by a poor, underemployed population. The scale of poverty and underemployment certainly suggests that Kilkenny was a fertile breeding ground for crime but the reality can only be understood through a detailed examination of the cases that actually appeared before the local courts. The following two chapters will examine the patterns of crime and sentencing in the city on the eve of the Famine in order to determine if the city was, in fact, as peaceful as the comments made in the courts at the time seem to imply.

2. Crime and sentencing in 1845

If contemporaries did not see an immediate connection between poverty and crime, part of the explanation may be the way in which crime was defined for statistical purposes and how the judicial system was administered. The framework of justice determined to some degree how, or if, someone would be punished and what degree of punishment would be handed out and hence shaped the view of contemporaries on the scale of criminal activity. In terms of criminal justice there were three types of court that sat locally: the petty sessions, the quarter sessions/city court and the assizes. These courts were part of the national framework of the justice system and are outlined briefly below. Kilkenny also had some local courts, a mayor's court, a sheriff's court, a market court, a court of conscience and a separate court in Irishtown, a portreeves court, that dealt exclusively with small debts and issued a process called *distringas*. *Distringas* was a process whereby goods to the value of 40*s*. were seized in lieu of fines issued at this court.

THE NATIONAL FRAMEWORK OF JUSTICE

By the start of the 19th century there were a number of superior courts in Ireland. These included the 'four courts' of Chancery, King's Bench, Exchequer and Common Pleas. There was also a court of Admiralty and local diocesan courts which were basically an ecclesiastical court holding jurisdiction over testamentary matters, i.e., wills. Most of these courts had their origins in the medieval period.[1] The practice of the law was in the hands both of a professional class and a lesser group of gentry who acted as justices of the peace and magistrates. There was, however, a well-developed set of rules for the conduct of the criminal law that ensured that it operated in similar ways across the country. In the case of sentencing, for example, there were several contemporary volumes that summarized the various statutes covering criminal law that would have been used on a national and local level. They detailed the minimum and maximum sentences available for specific crimes.[2] These volumes laid out the guidelines for sentencing, but as evidenced below, there was a certain leeway given in some cases.

The three local courts of most concern to Kilkenny were the courts of petty sessions, quarter sessions and the assizes, where most business was done. The courts of petty sessions had their formal origin in an act of 1827[3] but a form of petty sessions was held in both Kildare and Meath as early as 1810.[4] This reform of the magistracy and the formalization of the practice of justices of the peace sitting over minor cases at a local level was part of an ongoing reform of the Irish legal and judicial system starting with the Peace Preservation Act of 1814 and the establishment of the county constabularies in 1822. There were a number of reasons that encouraged central government to set up petty sessions. The petty sessions act was intended to encourage people to use the law. Before the act, the quarter sessions were prohibitively expensive for the lower classes and the alternative to quarter sessions was seeking the aid of a local magistrate who could act on behalf of the suitor. This depended on the benevolence of the magistrate who was often a local landlord. He could, if necessary, seek information and have the case sent to quarter sessions or the assizes if relevant.[5] Since the magistrates acted in private, accusations of bias or elements of coercion were possible. By moving these minor cases into the public domain through the petty sessions it gave justice a more visible profile. It also held the magistrates and justices of the peace, who mostly gave judgment without a jury, more accountable for their actions.

The petty sessions act of 1827 allowed for the appointment of a clerk for each of the courts or districts set up. He was responsible for charging the fee set out in the act for bringing a case forward and with keeping a registry book (fig. 3). He was also accountable for keeping legal documents, getting them signed by at least two magistrates and seeing that they were sent monthly to the clerk of the crown or peace of his respective county. The petty sessions court was modified by an act of 1836 but in 1845 its activities were still regulated by the 1827 act until the significant reforms of 1851 (parts of which are still in use today).[6] The jurisdiction of the petty sessions courts covered a wide range of offences and included 'wages, conditions of work, workers' combinations and unlawful societies or assembly, weights and measures, the licensing and operation of public houses, cruelty to animals, salvage, trespass, poaching (fish, game), forcible entry, malicious injury, simple assault and the poor law and workhouses'.[7] A number of these offences were dealt with at the petty sessions in Kilkenny in 1845. One point of note is that there are few parliamentary papers recording the statistics for crimes tried at petty sessions in contrast to statistics gathered for crimes at the assizes and quarter sessions, and this may reflect something of the attitude of contemporaries to the sort of minor offences that appeared before the petty sessions as opposed to what they regarded as the more significant crime that the quarter sessions dealt with. There are statistics available for 1842 and from 1845 onwards and there are also some published accounts at a local level of fines at petty sessions from 1840.[8] These allow for an examination of the fines and give an indication if those from later sessions were the norm or the exception.

SCHEDULE OF FEES.

	s.	*d.*
Summons and Copy - - - - -	0	6
Warrant , - - - - - -	0	6
Recognizance - - - - - -	1	0
Conviction - - - - - - -	1	0
Engrossing Information in Assaults, Trespasses, and all Mis- } demeanors - - - - - - }	1	0
Appeal to Quarter Sessions - - - - -	1	6
Supersedeas - - - - - -	0	6

3. Copy of the schedule of fees from the petty sessions act of 1827.

Sentencing at petty sessions normally consisted of a fine or a short term of imprisonment. An important function of the petty sessions courts was to conduct 'a preliminary examination of criminals who were to be tried on assize'.[9] The magistrate had to decide if there was enough evidence and then either discharge the accused or send him to trial at quarter sessions or assize. If he was sent for trial a 'bill of indictment' was set out and presented to the grand jury. They then had to decide if it was a 'true bill' and if so it 'became an indictment' and was subsequently tried at quarter sessions or assizes.[10] This process is often referred in the newspapers as 'ordering informations'.

Above the courts of petty sessions were the courts of quarter sessions, which were reserved for more serious crimes. Quarter sessions had their origins in several acts of the 14th century when they were originally established in England. The practice of sitting four times a year began in 1414. It is not known when exactly this practice came to be the norm in Ireland. Larceny over a certain value, assault, accessory to felony, rescue, running a house of ill-repute were all crimes that appeared before the magistrates at the quarter sessions in Kilkenny City in 1845.[11] The assistant barrister of the county was the official in charge of prosecutions at the quarter sessions as the offences at these courts required a greater understanding of the law than those at petty sessions. In contrast to the courts of petty sessions, the quarter sessions were always held in public places.

At the top of the local judicial tree was the assize court. In Ireland from the beginning of the 17th century the practice of judges going out from Dublin on an assize circuit was put in place, a system that continues to this day. There were six such circuits by 1845 with Kilkenny being part of the Leinster circuit.[12] Assize courts were usually reserved for the most serious crimes. Rape, bigamy, assault and larceny were all heard at the city assizes in 1845. In Kilkenny city they were held in conjunction with the quarter sessions and thus sat four times a year. Assizes were also normally presided over by a judge of king's bench, a number of magistrates and an official referred to as either a court recorder or chairman depending on the time period. The court recorder was the highest ranking judge present and had the title of baron. Baron Pennefeather and Baron Lefroy were the judges at the assizes for 1845. In 1845 cases that would normally have been heard at the summer quarter sessions were instead heard at the assizes. This was because of a jurisdictional problem resulting from the municipal corporations act and the lack of a recorder for the court.[13]

Cases at quarter sessions and assizes were tried by jury instead of the verdict being decided on by the bench, after the case was put forward by the plaintiff and the defendant as was normally the case at petty sessions.[14] Counsel was often present at the assizes, mostly due to the seriousness of an assize trial and the potential severity of the sentences. Offences warranting capital punishment or transportation for life – initially murder or treason, and by 1845 extending to Whiteboy offences, robbery of arms and other more serious breaches of the law,[15] including cases of serious assault or violent indecent assault – were passed over from the quarter sessions to the assizes on the various circuits.[16] Grand juries, composed of freeholders from the county who had local administrative and taxation functions, were also involved at the assize sessions. When the judge or assistant barrister gave his address to the court they were charged with finding the bill to be 'true' and whether it warranted being heard or not.[17] The grand jury usually consisted of 23 individuals. There was a property qualification and a monetary qualification to be a member. A vote by at least twelve jurors was then required for the bill to be found 'true'.[18]

The petty sessions, quarter sessions and assizes were the most important of the city courts and are the focus of the final chapter of this book. There are, however, four more courts that warrant mentioning, as they still sat in the city in the period under study. The mayor's court was responsible for minor affairs – mostly small matters of disputes between employers and employees and other very minor matters. This court still sat in 1845. There was only one reference to this court in the newspapers in 1845 when a city official was charged by a city constable with obstructing the course of justice.[19] The market court was responsible for dealing with irregularities noticed in the city markets. Matters that arose included weights being incorrect, meat on sale being spoiled and other such commercial items. There were numerous references in the newspapers to sittings of the market court in 1845. A court of conscience was a court established for the recovery of small debts; in Irishtown this was styled as the portreeve's court. This court had responsibility for dealing with disputes where the sum involved was less than 40s. Processes issued for this court were referred to as *distringas*, which was issued when the debt was not forthcoming. It allowed for bailiffs to seize property unless the debt was fulfilled. This method was rarely resorted to.[20] There were several references to this process in 1845.[21]

All this judicial system imposed a cost on local society. It is possible to at least partially reconstruct the cost of both administering and maintaining the criminal justice system in the city through an analysis of the grand jury minute books for the city, the parliamentary papers and the local newspapers. Excluding the fees paid to magistrates and some other court officials the cost to the rate payer for 1845 came to £1,369 9s. 9d. Tables 4 and 5 below show the breakdown of this cost.[22]

Table 4. Approximate cost of administering the legal system in the city in 1845, taken from the grand jury assize books, Spring 1845

Spring assizes			
Expense	*£*	*s.*	*d.*
Deputy clerk of the crown	37	0	0
Clerk of the peace	46	10	0
Secretary to the grand jury	18	10	0
Sheriff of the grand jury	12	0	0
Judge's crier	2	10	0
Courthouse keeper	5	0	0
Coals and candles for the courthouse	3	0	0
Bread, milk and coals for the prisoners	80	0	0
Physician and surgeon to the gaol	15	0	0
Gaol inspector	15	0	0
Apothecary to the gaol	4	15	7
Governor's salary	42	10	0
First turnkey	12	10	0
Second turnkey	12	10	0
Parson's salary	15	0	0
RC chaplain's salary	15	0	0
Matron's salary	7	10	0
Constabulary salaries	283	13	1
Re-imbursement of salaries	20	0	0
Rent for part of the courthouse	2	10	0
Minister's money	2	10	0
Advertising in the *Moderator*	5	0	0
Advertising in the *Journal*	5	0	0
Total for Spring assizes	**662**	**18**	**8**

Evidence of what the inhabitants of Kilkenny thought about these costs for the administration of justice is rather thin. The costs of the constabulary, for instance, were paid for by the cess raised on the city by the city grand jury. In 1845, however, the corporation discussed the need to write to the lord

Table 5. Approximate cost of administering the legal system in the city in 1845, taken from the grand jury assize books, Summer 1845

Summer assizes			
Expense	£	*s.*	*d.*
Money advanced to witnesses	6	10	0
Inquests	12	0	0
Deputy clerk of the crown	37	0	0
Clerk of the peace	46	10	0
Secretary to the grand jury	18	10	0
Sheriff of the grand jury	12	0	0
Judge's crier	2	10	0
Courthouse keeper	5	0	0
Coals and candles for the courthouse	5	0	0
Bread, milk and coals for the prisoners	200	0	0
Physician and surgeon to the gaol	15	0	0
Gaol inspector	15	0	0
Apothecary to the gaol	3	13	10
Governor's salary	42	10	0
First turnkey	12	10	0
Second turnkey	12	10	0
Parson's salary	15	0	0
RC chaplain's salary	15	0	0
Matron's salary	7	10	0
Advertising in the *Moderator*	6	4	0
Advertising in the *Journal*	4	16	3
Constabulary salaries	210	17	0
Total for Summer assizes	705	11	1
Grand Total	1,369	9	9

lieutenant asking that the expense of the constabulary be transferred from the local authority to central government.[23] Whatever the cost, the administration of justice was the basis on which property rights could be protected and law and order maintained and while the grand jury assessment may not have been paid willingly, it was paid. The pattern of sentencing revealed in the next chapter shows how important contemporaries thought the justice system was; sentencing was carefully calibrated in an effort to maintain social order through the protection of public and private property and the public peace. The criminal justice system succeeded in maintaining order in the potentially disordered city of Kilkenny in 1845 and for that a price had to be paid.

Most of those who broke the law in Kilkenny and were caught found themselves before the petty sessions, the quarter sessions or the assize, depending on the seriousness of the offence. Petty sessions sat fortnightly and account for the bulk of criminal activity in the city in 1845. For Kilkenny the assizes and quarter sessions sat in conjunction. The assizes sat twice in the city in 1845 with the quarter sessions sitting three times, due to the jurisdictional issue previously mentioned. For the purpose of the relevant parliamentary statistics, quarter sessions and assizes were recorded together. This is despite the fact that there were specific offences that should have been heard at each of these courts. A list of crimes that warranted being heard at an assize court as opposed to a court of quarter sessions allows for a breakdown of this amalgamation of statistics. This material forms the basis for an analysis of the patterns of crime, and the reactions of the courts to that crime in the form of sentencing in pre-Famine Kilkenny. When taken with the discussion of the social context of that crime, this allows a reconstruction of criminal activities in Kilkenny in 1845, which forms the basis of the next chapter.

3. Crime and sentencing in Kilkenny city in 1845

As the previous chapter suggests, Kilkenny in 1845 had a well-developed judicial infrastructure that was a local manifestation of a system that functioned on a national level. While the detection of crime was a more haphazard process, its prosecution and punishing was something understood by most in Kilkenny. Few in the city in 1845 could not have been unaware of, and probably had been in contact with, the judicial processes in the town. The petty sessions reached deep into local societies and dealt with minor infractions of the law, while the higher courts of quarter sessions and assizes had attached to them a pomp that few could have avoided as the assize judges came to town. Once one had fallen into the hands of the judicial system one's treatment was not random. Patterns of trial and sentencing reflected the social attitudes and priorities of those on the judicial bench and hence provides a way of revealing the fears and priorities of the social elite of Kilkenny in 1845. By looking at patterns of conviction and sentencing this chapter will explore some of those fears and priorities.

PETTY SESSIONS

Of all the courts operating in Kilkenny city in 1845, the petty sessions are the most important since they dealt with the most common offences in the city. The court of petty sessions sat at least once a month in the courthouse above the city gaol in Kilkenny. It followed a set procedure that usually involved the plaintiff and the defendant in turn presenting their case to the lay magistrate on the bench. At least two justices of the peace/resident magistrates sat for these sessions. The mayor was normally one of these, alongside another local magistrate. Until June 1845 the mayor was Robert Cane; then Edmond Smithwick was elected. The other resident magistrate was normally Joseph Greene although Richard Sullivan frequently sat at these sessions as well. The marquess of Ormonde also attended at one sitting of the petty sessions in November 1845.[1] The clerk of the peace was also present and he was charged with recording the proceedings and keeping a record of the fines and the sentences. There is evidence from both of the local newspapers for the presence of legal counsel at these sessions in Kilkenny city. This is supported by the studies of both McCabe and McMahon, which show that the use of attorneys was widespread at petty sessions in Mayo and Galway prior to the Famine.[2] Attorneys – likely barristers or solicitors, the term is not clearly defined – were generally available to hire at a cost of approximately 2s. 6d. and presented the case to the bench for the benefit of their client. The fee of a half crown was a relatively large amount of money for the lower classes and when combined with the fee of 6d. to issue the summons this would amount to a total of 3s., which is the equivalent of at least three to five days wages for a labourer. Despite this, and the relatively small fines levied, attorneys were still used. Cases where they were employed mostly concerned poor rates where a group of individuals employed an attorney to act on their behalf.[3] Attorneys were also employed for the more serious cases, theft above a certain value and assault, for example.[4] Apart from winning the case there was no obvious benefit to such a substantial outlay on an attorney. It may have come down to a matter of prestige to have a case won at petty sessions on a point of law and this may suggest that some legal proceedings were as much about local senses of honour as about the rights and wrongs of a case.

The punishment handed down at petty sessions was normally a fine or a short term of imprisonment. Cases could be brought by anyone who could pay the fees set out in figure 3 above, along with the sum of 6d. necessary for a summons. Cases were often brought by the local constabulary and the local poor law rate collector. Many individuals brought to petty sessions by the constabulary were charged with relatively trivial offences such as minor assaults or various breaches of the law that the city constabulary encountered on their daily duties. Figure 4 below shows the number of cases heard at petty sessions over the period 1845–50, and illustrates a dramatic increase in the number of cases heard over the course of the Famine when minor crime increased as a result of social tensions.

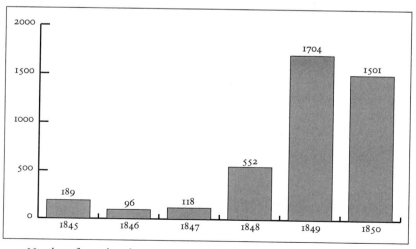

4. Number of cases heard at petty sessions in Kilkenny city between 1845 and 1850, compiled from the return of criminal offenders.[5]

For 1845 it was possible to get evidence by examining the newspapers for 111 individuals involved in a total of 97 cases that came up before the petty sessions court. Often multiple persons were tried for the same offence; in instances like these the number of individuals is noted but it is treated as one case in the appendix, hence the figure of 97 cases and 111 individuals. This amounts to almost half of the total number of cases recorded in parliamentary returns, 189 in all, heard at petty sessions that year. The appendix gives more detail on each of the cases with the names of those involved and the summaries of the trial. The newspapers did not go into detail on every case. It was common for them to state that 'the other cases brought forward on this day were unimportant' where there was a significant number of cases on the calendar.[6] Also where a case took up a significant part of the day's business, and the court was adjourned, the papers may not have reported on the adjourned cases in their next edition.[7] By far the most common cases at these sessions were minor assaults and failure to pay poor rates. These account for 60 of the 97 cases that it was possible to reconstruct. The usual sentence in these cases was a small fine or a brief term of imprisonment. There were, however, crimes that proved exceptions to this; examples include assault on or by city officials or by people in a position of authority, criminal damage and theft of foodstuffs. These are discussed below.

ASSAULT AND CRIMINAL DAMAGE

Of the 21 cases of assault before the petty sessions for which evidence is available the sentences varied considerably. In terms of sentencing, the magistrates had several options. They could issue a fine, a short term of imprisonment, or bind the defendant to the peace. If the case was serious enough they could 'order information' and send the case to be heard at quarter sessions or assizes. Eleven of the defendants were ordered to keep the peace or committed to bail and released. A fine of 5s., or four days' to a week's imprisonment in lieu of payment, was handed down in three further cases. Two other cases resulted in fines of between 1s. and 2s. 6d. or 24 to 48 hours' imprisonment if no payment was forthcoming.[8] In a further two cases information was ordered and the cases were sent to the next quarter sessions. These were not minor skirmishes but more serious assaults, one for assault with a hammer and the second for forcibly breaking into a house and attempting to remove a child.[9] Of these 18 cases, most appear to have occurred between the ordinary citizens of the city, no occupations are given nor are addresses forthcoming so it is impossible to say much about their social circumstances. The sentencing and fines issued seem to have been typical for this type of crime and are similar to the published summaries of crimes found in the Kilkenny newspapers in earlier years, such as a published account of March 1840.[10]

The remaining cases, while still falling under the jurisdiction of the court of petty sessions, had larger fines and more severe custodial sentences imposed. The first of these was an unusual case. It involved two young boys, John Dunn and James Comerford, who extinguished a gas light with a piece of paper containing gunpowder in a shop on John Street. They were found guilty and fined 6*d*. and 1*s*. respectively, with sentences of 12 and 24 hours' imprisonment in lieu of the fines not being paid.[11] Why the fines were high in this case is unclear but the presence of gunpowder in the case may have caused concern on the bench. The remaining cases of damage present a rather different sort of problem. The first two cases involved James Sheehan and James Rawlins and they warranted fines of £1 with one week's hard labour and two weeks' imprisonment respectively, while the third, the case of John McDonald, resulted in a fine of £2 or one month's imprisonment. Why were these sentences so disproportionate to the other 18? As suggested above the answer lies in the nature of the victims of the assaults and also on the severity of the assault. James Sheehan, for example, was found to have been drunk and riotous. He resisted arrest and assaulted several of the city constables while James Rawlins assaulted a turnkey in the city gaol.[12] The last case involved an assault by a city constable, John McDonald, on a citizen.[13] It would appear that more serious assaults on, or indeed by, city officials were treated more severely than assaults on or by the ordinary citizenry, suggesting an anxiety about the authority of civic officials. A minor assault on a constable in October and another minor assault on a soldier by a drunk in January received lesser fines.[14] It remains to be seen if these instances of more severe sentencing were the norm or the exception; a study of sentencing over a longer period may help to answer these questions.

There is some further evidence from the petty sessions to back up the supposition that offences against authority or a place or position of authority could be treated more severely than mere brawling or minor damage. Michael O'Brien was charged by the master of the workhouse with criminal damage, having broken windows in the workhouse after being ejected from it due to him being fit for work. He had deliberately broken the windows in order to be sent to gaol or to be re-admitted to the workhouse as he was unable to find any work. William Green, one of the local magistrates on the day, commented that he could be given a fine of £5 or two months' imprisonment.[15] Sentencing was put off until the next sitting of the petty sessions to allow the board of guardians to meet and decide what they wanted to do in this matter. At the next meeting of the board of guardians they decided that 'the law should take its course' even after hearing the extenuating circumstances behind the crime. A comment was also made that 'the magistrates had no right to throw responsibility from themselves upon the board; he would be for telling them to deal with the man as they considered proper and do their duty'.[16] By the time of the next petty sessions in September the meeting of the board of guardians had been reported in the newspapers and the magistrate commented that 'the courtesy which had been manifested by the bench was not met with corresponding courtesy by the Board'; they were not pleased at what they saw as discourtesy and interference.

O'Brien eventually agreed to pay for the damages and the fine was reduced to a penny or an hour's imprisonment. It is possible that the extenuating circumstances behind O'Brien's crime led to this lessening of the sentence or that the comments made by the board of guardians regarding the magistrates were seen as inappropriate or offensive to the bench and the magistrates deliberately commuted the sentence to a much lesser one.

LARCENY AND THEFT

There were two cases of larceny or theft, both involving food, that resulted in severe sentences. The first case, reported on 8 January 1845, involved the theft of heads of cabbage reserved for seed by a resident of John Street, John McCraith. The witnesses called named the three culprits as Peggy Grace, Mary Grace and Betty Bryan. They were seen taking the seed cabbage but persuaded the witnesses not to disclose their presence. A summons was issued for their arrest with the magistrate commenting that they were liable to a fine of £20 or six months' imprisonment.[17] The second case involved the theft of potatoes. Anne Downes, Margaret Magrath and Catherine Murphy were found guilty of stealing from a Richard Magrath and 'after a most impressive admonition from the mayor' were given a sentence of one month's imprisonment with every second day being at hard labour.[18]

Whether it is a coincidence or not both of these cases involved women. Given that the role of women was usually a domestic one it is possible that they were stealing food in order to provide for their families. Unfortunately, the detail given for these cases in the newspapers does not provide enough information to make a judgment. No attorneys are mentioned as being present to defend the women in the second case, possibly they were unable to afford the necessary fee. Cases where attorneys were present seem to have warranted more attention in the newspapers as legal arguments were undoubtedly put forward for the defence, which made for better reporting compared to the sparse account given regarding the theft of the potatoes. Larceny, such as the theft of foodstuff, was taken very seriously and sentencing was correspondingly severe at both the quarter sessions and the petty sessions. Minor assaults, an attack on the person, warranted minor fines and brief terms of imprisonment but larceny, an attack on property, was sentenced much more severely. One further example to support the idea that criminal damage to public property, or damage to property in public places, was dealt with severely is provided by the instance of two boys 'of about seventeen years of age' who were arrested by a constable for cutting trees on the canal walk. They were sentenced to one week's imprisonment with hard labour.[19] These cases illustrate the deviation of punishments from the norm at petty sessions with regard to these type of crimes. The heaviest punishments were handed out because the crime was against personal property or involved city officials or city property. A similar pattern was evident at cases dealt with at the quarter sessions and assizes.

In contrast with the monthly sittings of the court of petty sessions, the court of quarter sessions usually sat four times a year, normally in March, June, October and November. In 1845, the Easter sessions for the city were delayed and cases normally heard at quarter sessions were tried at the assizes in July. This was due to a jurisdictional dispute about the role of county barristers and the county of the city of Kilkenny after the redrawing of the boundaries in 1840.[20] There was also a sitting of the quarter sessions in January instead of the previous March. The assize sessions were presided over by a professional judge and either Baron Pennefeather or Baron Lefroy who sat on the Queen's Bench, and the assistant barrister (N.P. O'Gorman). They were assisted by the mayor, Edmond Smithwick, as well as a number of magistrates, usually Robert Greene, and also many of the magistrates who sat at petty sessions. Judges of assizes were also responsible for hearing appeals from the assistant barrister's decisions.[21] The quarter sessions and assizes lasted up to five days and followed a set pattern. Cases of ejectment, replevin (a legal means for a person to recover goods unlawfully withheld from his or her possession) and legacy, along with all other civil bills, had to be registered or entered with the clerk of the peace on the day before the sessions sat. Civil cases were always heard first and were listed in alphabetical order. Cases of ejectment were normally heard on either the first or second day, with registration of voters being the first matter of business. The grand and petit juries were required to attend by ten o'clock on the first day of sitting. The grand jury decided if the cases before them were valid and warranted trial at the quarter sessions. Trial was by jury and juries were selected by a property qualification of £10 on freehold property or £15 on leasehold property – the lists of qualified jurors were compiled at the October sessions. This system was open to abuse and not everyone who met the qualification was on the jury list. Evidence in the *Report on the state of Ireland in respect of crime* in 1839 provides further detail on this system.[22] The property qualification was far above what the average person was earning each year and raises questions about possible class divides between the jurors and the poorer accused. A leasehold qualification of £15 was just over seven times higher than the average rent in towns and villages of £2, and 50 per cent higher than the average rent of an acre of conacre ground. The business then moved on to the granting of licences for spirits, beers and ales and also licences to keep firearms, which were granted after the applicants had received a recommendation from a magistrate at the petty sessions. Following this, and after the grand jury was sworn, appeals from magistrates' decisions, which were probably appeals from petty sessions, were heard followed by anyone appealing a fine and debtors 'applying under the Gaol act'.[23] Those involved in the individual cases, usually referred to as prosecutors and traversers, were required to attend on the second day at ten o'clock while defences were heard on or before noon on the second day of business. The last order of business were appeals to the barrister – these were always heard on the last day. The quarter sessions were, therefore, a much more complicated affair than the petty sessions and played a very important part in city life.

There were 54 people tried before the city quarter sessions and assizes in 1845. In a similar manner to that used for the petty sessions it was possible to reconstruct the cases for 45 of these individuals. In total there is evidence in the newspapers for the trials of 24 men and 21 women. No gender is specified for five further cases. In a number of instances several people were indicted for the same crime – when this is taken into account significant evidence remains for 35 cases. In contrast to the petty sessions a larger body of statistical material exists for the returns of committals at quarter sessions and assizes. Statistics for crime, sentencing and committals at the quarter sessions and assizes are drawn from two parliamentary papers: the annual returns of persons committed to gaols for trial and the annual returns of criminal offenders committed for trial.[24] There is some discrepancy between these papers. In some instances there were higher numbers committed to the city gaol than there were people returned in the statistics for committal to trial. There are several reasons for this. One is that for 1845 and 1846 the returns of committals to gaol for trial separates the city and the county of the city into different sections (the returns are based solely on the county of the city for 1847 to 1850), while in contrast the return of those committed for trial for all this period uses the county of the city exclusively as the geographical area for the statistical returns. Other possible reasons for the discrepancies in the numbers include the returns of the assizes. These were cases tried before the crown solicitor on circuit, and they account for 16 of the cases in 1845 for the county of the city.[25] Further possible reasons include the fact that the statistics were compiled annually so that someone who was committed to gaol for trial late in a particular year could conceivably end up in the statistics for two separate years.[26] Tables 6 and 7 show the numbers of committals, indictments, convictions and discharges or acquittals for Kilkenny city gaol for 1845, while the sentencing and relevant details are also given. For 1845 the numbers of cases reported in both newspapers and the parliamentary returns are the same. The appendix provides more details on the cases held at the quarter sessions and assizes. Using these statistics it was possible to chart the levels of recorded crime over a ten-year period and to see if the Famine and the resulting deprivation resulted in an increase of the levels of recorded crime (figs 5 and 6).

Table 6. Numbers of committals, indictments, convictions and those discharged for Kilkenny city gaol for 1845, taken from the return of committals[27]

Crimes	Committals	Indictments	Convictions	Acquitted or discharged
Assault	3	2	2	1
Bigamy	1	1	1	0
House-breaking	2	2	2	0
Larceny	25	20	14	11
Perjury	1	1	0	1
Receiving stolen goods	9	9	3	6
Rescuing	4	4	1	3
Uttering counterfeit coin	2	2	2	0
Accessory to felony	3	3	3	0
Indecent exposure	1	1	0	1
Fraud	1	1	0	1
Keeping a house of ill fame	2	2	0	2
Total	**54**	**48**	**28**	**26**

Note: six instances of committal did not lead to indictment.

Table 7. Numbers of convictions and type of sentence handed down for Kilkenny city gaol for 1845

Crime for which convicted	No. convicted	Transportation	Imprisonment
Assault	2		2
Bigamy	1		1
Uttering counterfeit coin	2	1	1
House-breaking	2		2
Larceny	14	2	12
Accessory to felony	3		3
Receiving stolen goods	3	2	1
Rescuing	1		1
Total	**28**	**5**	**23**

An analysis of the number of people committed compared with the number of cases heard at these sessions over the period 1845 to 1850 shows similar trends (figs 5 and 6). From a relative low in 1845 there is a sharp increase, peaking in 1848, before decreasing after this point. Looking at the numbers of cases at quarter sessions and assizes in the appendix it is immediately obvious that the most prevalent type of criminal offence brought before the courts was for

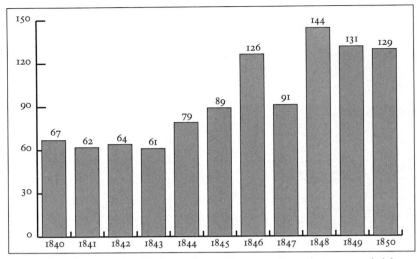

5. Number of committals in Kilkenny city gaol between 1840 and 1850, compiled from the statistics for the committals to the city gaol from the city and county of the city at first, and then from the county of the city only.

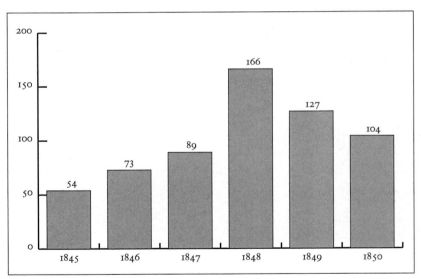

6. Number of cases heard at quarter sessions and assizes in the city between 1845 and 1850.[28]

larceny. Cases of larceny accounted for 25 of the 54 cases, with indictments following for 20 of these, with 14 convictions. The second-largest classification of offence was for receiving stolen goods where there was 9 committals with

3 convictions. The various other types of crimes account for the remaining 11 convictions.

Evidence from the newspapers provides details of the cases and the sentencing for 12 of the convictions for larceny, while parliamentary papers provide details of the sentencing for the remaining two cases. In nine instances the sentence handed down was a term of imprisonment for six months or less, in three further cases the sentence was for between six months and one year, with seven years' transportation being handed down in the remaining two cases. Periodic solitary confinement or occasional spells of hard labour were also used in sentencing these convicts. There is significant variation in the sentencing, which can be explained by the specific nature of the larcenies. Certain kinds of larceny were treated more harshly than others, just as assaults or criminal damage involving people or places in authority or theft of personal property were treated more severely at the petty sessions. There is, therefore, a similarity in the pattern of sentencing at these sessions to the sentencing at the petty sessions where theft of, or repeated theft of, personal property was treated harshly. Recidivism, or repeat offending, was seen in a negative light and was sentenced severely.

The three harshest terms of confinement were all given to women for the theft of personal property or money. These were for 9–12 months with four days' solitary confinement every six weeks for two of them and a sentence of nine months, commuted from seven years' transportation, for the third. In the first instance Anastasia Hackett and Margaret Shearman, two 'nymphs of the pave', were charged with the theft of a tobacco box containing £1 and 6d., even though the prosecutor could not prove that the money belonged to his client. The women were noted as being 'persons of previously disreputable character' when they were sentenced which, given the length of the sentence, supports the supposition that repeat offending or perceptions of a disorderly life was harshly punished.[29] A reference to Catherine Ryan as being a 'habitual thief' prior to her sentence of six months with three days' hard labour and solitary confinement every six weeks also lends some credence to this theory. One other severe sentence, that of seven years' transportation (but later commuted), was for theft of a gown and a petticoat by Bridget Flynn. A similar case heard on the same day for the theft of a cloak only received a five-month sentence.[30] It seems likely that it was because Flynn stole two items, she was punished severely – but on consideration the assistant barrister commuted the sentence. Nevertheless, it was within his remit to transport her for stealing the two items of clothing. Theft of multiple items seems to have been treated considerably more harshly than theft of a single item; who she stole the items from may also have been a relevant factor.

This is also clear in the two cases of larceny that resulted in sentences of transportation. Both of these were for stealing multiple items and in both cases pawning the stolen articles for money. Elizabeth Hearne was transported for seven years for stealing 9 yards of calico, 12 yards of cashmere, a shawl and other articles from a shop on High Street. She had repeatedly been in the shop over a period of a few weeks and stole the materials, which she then pawned for money. When she was arrested she had the tickets from the pawnbroker on her person.[31] The second instance of larceny resulting in transportation was that of John Fitzgerald, a 14-year-old from Tipperary. He was tried twice at the October sessions. His first conviction was for being in possession of stolen goods[32] and his second was for stealing a coat vest and flannel petticoat from a James Foley and pawning them for 6s. The mayor noted that the pawnbroker frequently approached him about 'suspicious characters'. In passing sentence the barrister stated that 'he was so matured in vice that it was impossible to hope for his improvement in this country' and 'that though young in years, he was old in iniquity'.[33] In both instances the stolen property was recovered yet the sentence of transportation was still handed down; it is possible that these sentences were severe in order to serve as a warning to the community. The remaining eight cases of larceny resulted in sentences of four to six months and were handed down for offences varying from stealing a sack to stealing clothes. The single case of house-breaking involved two individuals, Richard Walsh and Thomas Quirk, who were convicted of breaking into a storehouse on Green Street. They were observed leaving the garden of the storehouse by one witness and it was on this basis and on the fact that Head Constable Lynn matched the footprints in the garden to the accused that they were convicted. In sentencing them to 12 months' imprisonment the assistant barrister commented that 'he was unable to sentence them to transportation, as he would wish to have done', as they broke into a storehouse rather than a dwelling house.[34] Again, the harsher sentence available was for an offence committed against an individual's personal property, in this instance a house. The sentencing pattern here was similar to the harsher sentencing already seen for more serious assaults on individuals and for multiple thefts of personal property.

There were two cases of receiving stolen goods involving three individuals. James Conway was indicted for receiving a coat, a shirt, a sheet and 7s. 6d. from James Moran knowing that they were stolen. Constable Nathaniel Stuart returned the goods upon searching the house of the accused and he received a sentence of six months' imprisonment.[35] The second case involved a married couple, Sarah and James Moriarty, who were tried for receiving a piece of blue cloth; they were transported for seven years. At first glance there appears to be a significant discrepancy between the two sentences. The Moriartys were arrested in Waterford by a member of the local constabulary 'in consequence of having a suspicion of their character'; he found them to be in possession of a box containing cloth and 'other articles' and when he discovered they had come from Kilkenny they were returned there for trial. They were in possession of less than seven yards of cloth, which had been stolen in late July or August. The owner of the shop and his assistant both gave evidence as to the value of the cloth and the fact that it was a relatively rare piece.[36] It seems that in conjunction with being in possession of a number of items it was the value of the cloth and its unique character that led to the sentence of transportation. The assistant barrister did, however, refer the final decision on the sentence to the law officers of the crown, who either represented the attorney general or the judges on assize. Sarah Moriarty wrote a memorial to the lord lieutenant pleading for clemency but the file is not available. The fact that she is included in the transportation registers suggests that her appeal was unsuccessful.[37]

ASSAULT

Of the three cases of assault two led to convictions. These were for assault with intent to ravish (which was the act of forcibly carrying a woman away with intent to force sexual relations) by John Bryan, for which he was sentenced to six months' imprisonment, and an assault by John Connors, for which he received four months.[38] These sentences are relatively consistent and reflect the pattern seen in the sentencing of assaults at petty sessions. The cases were treated seriously and the sentence reflected how the magistrates, or in this case the assistant barrister, viewed the specific details of the assault, with the lengthier sentence handed down to the assault with intent to ravish, this case being seen as the more serious of the two.

OTHER OFFENCES

The single instance of bigamy resulted in a 12-month sentence for Stephen Flanigan who two years previously had abandoned his wife and children. It was, interestingly, a case of double bigamy as his second wife had also left her husband but had absconded on the morning of the trial rather than face prosecution. He was brought to trial by someone who happened to be at his first wedding and having been made aware of his second brought it to the attention of the constabulary.[39] Rescue was the act of being freed or of freeing oneself from the custody of an officer of the law or of reclaiming goods taken or awarded under a civil bill. Of the four indictments for rescue at quarter sessions there was just one conviction for which Richard Saunders received a sentence of two weeks' imprisonment.[40]

What makes the single instance of counterfeiting at the Kilkenny assizes unusual is that it occurred in the city gaol and led to the lord lieutenant ordering the grand jury to hold an inquiry in relation to alleged misconduct by the governor of the gaol, thus generating a considerable amount of evidence. The case involved two individuals both of whom were repeat offenders, Patrick Ronan and William Russell, who were 'day men' in the gaol. Ronan was indicted for having in his possession five counterfeit shillings and was already on a charge of intending to rob the constabulary after he lost razors he was meant to repair in Carrick. He was also under a sentence of transportation but the assistant barrister had tried that case without the jurisdiction to do so and it was deemed illegal. For his part in the counterfeiting he was sentenced to two years' hard labour. Russell, who had been a private of the 14th dragoons, was indicted for having made 10 penny pieces of counterfeit coin. He was convicted on the evidence of other prisoners and Head Constable Lynn and was sentenced to transportation for seven years. The variation in the sentencing seems significantly different and comes down to the fact that Ronan was mistakenly indicted for having the base coin in his possession whereas Russell was indicted for actually producing it. The severe sentences were a combination of both men being repeat offenders, the seriousness of the crime and where it was committed.[41]

There was one case of, and three convictions for, accessory to felony, essentially having knowledge of, or planning, but not participating in the crime itself. Joseph Phelan, Catherine Power and Patrick Kelly were convicted for inciting Ellen Dunn to steal three bank notes to the sum of £14 10s., the property of Edward Lalor. Dunn worked as a servant to the Lalor family and over a period of a few months the accused persuaded her to steal money. They finally stole the money from a lockbox with the aid of a forged key. Dunn was overheard trying to persuade them to give the money back and it was on this basis that the crime was discovered. The jury returned a guilty verdict despite the fact that the accused had numerous witnesses to attest to their character. The assistant barrister warned them that it was within his power to sentence them to ten years' transportation but he deferred sentencing to give them time to reflect on their actions. They were eventually sentenced to six months' imprisonment but Patrick Kelly was freed after petitioning the lord lieutenant for clemency.[42]

It seems clear that the criminal justice system, at least as it was practised in Kilkenny in 1845, was not a random affair. Sentencing, whether at the minor petty sessions courts or the more serious assizes or quarter sessions, was carefully calibrated. Sentences reflected the social concerns and perceptions of the judicial officials at the various courts, representatives of the elite of society. Property required protection and hence the severest sentences were reserved for larceny or damage to public or private property. Sentences for assault were likewise calibrated according to the severity of the assault and the status of the victim. Perhaps most interesting was the concern with attacks, albeit minor ones, on the property of the state or on the agents of the state. Such concern to protect the position of state officials, even minor ones, with severe sentences says much about the fears and anxieties of those who lived in mid-19th-century Ireland.

Conclusion

The idea behind this short book was to examine crime and sentencing as a reflection of social and living conditions in Kilkenny city in 1845. The introductory chapters show that life in Kilkenny in 1845 was very much a tale of two cities. On the outside there were all the high value houses, the shops, banks and business premises that lined High Street, Parliament Street and Rose Inn Street, which would have presented an elegant facade to any visitor to the city. There were the local government buildings including the courthouse, the workhouse and the castle, all of which are, or in the case of the workhouse, were, imposing structures. Behind this veneer of high class respectability there was the other side to Kilkenny, a place of cramped low-value houses and relatively high unemployment, where petty crime and drunkenness were common, and for many people life was primarily one of subsistence. There was, however, awareness of the conditions of the lower classes both nationally and locally and efforts and measures were discussed to alleviate some of the burden felt by them. These measures included proposals towards providing an allotment system, as well as the construction of the workhouses, albeit based on the English model of poor law, instead of the model originally recommended. Living conditions were poor and there was already evidence to suggest an over-reliance on the potato as a crop. Rents were high and most people were unable to afford to buy food or other goods at markets, with the average yearly wage for the lower classes barely enough for rent and a minimum amount of food.

The question then is how were these levels of poverty reflected in the crimes heard before the courts of petty and quarter sessions. An examination of the crimes was made possible through an analysis of the newspapers and this shows that the predominant crimes were the theft of foodstuffs and clothing. Larceny and receiving stolen goods account for 34 of the 54 cases at quarter sessions or assizes in 1845, while assaults account for the highest amount of cases at petty sessions. There were also numerous references in the newspapers throughout the year to the increasing frequency of the theft of foodstuffs. There is a correlation between the poor living conditions and the theft of food and clothing. Drunkenness was also a considerable problem in the city with 376 people fined or committed for various breaches of the act governing drunkenness in public.[1]

The theory behind periods of confinement, as opposed to older forms of corporal punishment, was based on the principle of 'deprivation of liberty'.[2] The 18th and 19th centuries saw significant change in the legal system and also the construction of prisons with individual cells and the concept of a penal sentence being applied that 'makes it possible to quantify the penalty exactly according to the variable of time'.[3] Thus, the way in which society viewed specific crimes was reflected in the punishments. This is clear in the sentencing in Kilkenny in 1845 where it has been shown that the more severe sentences were handed down for theft of personal property, damage to personal property, particularly violent assault upon the person, damage to official property and to people in a position of power or authority breaching or misusing that power. This pattern is relatively consistent and is seen in the sentencing at petty sessions, quarter sessions and assizes. The harshest sentences at quarter sessions and assizes were reserved for thefts of personal items or were handed down for thefts of multiple items or repeat offending and for theft of food. The longest custodial sentences were handed down for house-breaking and for the incident of coining.

Recidivism, or the act of repeat offending, was treated severely. While first offences were not always treated leniently there appears to have been a certain amount of latitude granted to first-time offenders depending on the offence. This pattern was repeated in the sentencing at petty sessions. The most severe custodial terms at petty sessions were usually for one month's imprisonment. This sentence was handed down for a theft of potatoes, while an assault by a constable on a member of the public received a fine of £2 or a month's imprisonment in lieu of payment of the fine. A sentence of two months given at petty sessions for breaking windows in the workhouse was ultimately deferred but the harsh sentence was a possibility as it was a direct attack on public property.

Some of the issues that this book has raised clearly need further investigation. For example, the issue of jury selection is an area that needs be examined in greater detail. There was a substantial monetary qualification to be on the jury list. The result of this was that the middle classes dominated the jury list, while it seems to have been the lower classes who were those predominantly on trial. They were often faced with being judged and tried by wealthy magistrates while a jury of people above their social station were responsible for deciding their guilt or innocence.

Another point that warrants further analysis is the underlying principle behind the sentencing. As can be seen in the summaries of the trials in the appendix, numerous crimes seem to have been, in today's terms at least, very minor. What was the underlying principle behind the punishments? Were they deemed necessary to control the lower classes, or, to use larceny as an example, to make a point that personal property was to some extent inviolable and that theft was not to be tolerated?

It cannot be definitively stated that the high levels of unemployment and poor wages had a direct correlation with the incidences of larceny and theft of foodstuff, but with the cramped living conditions, large family sizes and the costs of goods at market it seems likely that they were significant contributing factors. The evidence of the poor law reports and that of Dr Cane certainly

7. Cottage at Butt's Cross, Kilkenny, *c.*1842, from Hall's *Ireland*, volume 2.

show that overcrowding and poor living conditions were prevalent in the city a decade prior to the study period. Despite these poor living conditions, overall crime levels in Kilkenny city were low. This is possibly due to low crime detection rates. With a population of approximately 19,066 there were only a mere 285 cases before the courts in 1845, excluding cases of drunkenness. This is only 1.49 per cent of the total population. Either the city was incredibly docile in spite of the evidence for poverty and overcrowding or a lot of crime simply went unpunished or unreported. The majority of cases at petty sessions were for failure to pay poor rates, with a relatively small number of cases for larceny and common assaults. The assizes and quarter sessions did not see any capital crimes or indeed any particularly serious crimes. Sentencing was, however, severe with five instances of transportation, four of which were for larceny or receiving stolen goods. Was severe sentencing a factor in these low levels of crime or were the levels of crime simply low anyway? Comments by the assistant barrister congratulating the grand jury on the quiet nature of their city would seem to suggest that crime in the city was indeed low and that the general population were docile.[4] The evidence of the courts presented above and in the appendix would certainly seem to support this.

Appendix

Name	Crime	Sentence	Details
Not given	3 cases of stealing potatoes, one of stealing a coat and one of stealing money	No details given	None given
Catherine Power, Joseph Phelan, Patrick Kelly	Accessory to felony	Convicted with a recommendation to mercy; sentence deferred for a few days	Assisted Ellen Dunn in stealing three bank notes to the sum of £14 10s., the property of Edward Lalor
John Millea	Debt	Ordered to pay within six months	Brought up to apply for his discharge. This was opposed by Anastasia Barlow to whom he owed money
Not given	Exposing her person	Case ignored	No details given
Ellen Dunn	Felony	Deferred	Stealing three bank notes to the sum of £14 10s., the property of Edward Lalor
Daniel Kelly	Forgery	Information ordered	Information was ordered. Case was sent to next quarter sessions. Kelly forged the signatures of Michael Cormack and Pierce Dowling on an IOU for £2
Terence Reilly	Fraud	Acquitted	Pretended to be deaf and dumb and skilled in healing diseases. Took money off Ellen Stapleton to buy a cure for her sick child and decamped with it
Catherine Brennan, James Gwynne, Mary Walsh	Keeping a house of ill fame	Informations were sworn at petty sessions	Mary Kealy charged Gwynne, Brennan and Walsh with keeping in Poyntz Lane improper houses and harbouring people of improper character to the public scandal and nuisance. Case adjourned to next quarter sessions

Name	Crime	Sentence	Details
Anastasia Macarthy	Larceny	Three months' imprisonment	Indicted for stealing a sack, the property of William Williams. Macarthy sold the sack to a Mary Mulhall for 4d. who gave the sack to Constable O'Hara. Prisoner was subsequently found drunk. Her husband was dead and she had 6 children
Catherine Ryan	Larceny	Six months, with three days' hard labour and solitary confinement each six weeks	Theft of ten stone of potatoes, property of Godfrey Greene, crime of exceedingly frequent occurrence
Patrick Guilfoyle	Larceny	Acquitted	Acquitted on stealing eight loads of stable manure
Thomas Landy	Larceny	Four months' imprisonment	Indicted for stealing five shirts and one waistcoat, the property of Lt Andrew Greene and one handkerchief, property of Philip Watt; evidence given as to good character; recommendation given to mercy
Eliza Kavanagh	Larceny	Acquitted	Indicted for stealing a brass candlestick, property of Anastasia Walsh
John Fitzgerald	Larceny	Transported for seven years	Indicted for stealing clothes from James Foley, a coat vest and flannel petticoat, Fitzgerald pawned the clothes for 6s. Barrister remarked that he was so matured in vice, so steeped in crime that it was impossible to hope for his improvement in this country. Fitzgerald was only 14
Anastasia Hackett	Larceny	Twelve months, with four days' solitary confinement each six weeks	Stealing a pound note and 1s. 6d. with a tobacco box. Sentenced as persons of previously disreputable character
Margaret Shearman	Larceny	Nine months, with four days' solitary confinement each six weeks	Stealing a pound note and 1s. 6d. with a tobacco box. Sentenced as persons of previously disreputable character
Sarah Moriarty, Owen Moriarty	Receiving stolen goods	Seven years' transportation	Indicted for receiving a piece of blue cloth knowing it to be stolen. Arrested by Constable John Spillane in Waterford

Name	Crime	Sentence	Details
James Conway	Receiving stolen goods	Six months' imprisonment	James Conway was indicted for stealing goods off James Moran – a coat, a shirt, a sheet and 7s. 6d. Constable Nathaniel Stuart returned the goods upon searching the house of the accused
Richard Saunders	Rescue	A fortnight's imprisonment	Guilty of rescue
Thomas Bibby	Rescue	Guilty, allowed to plead guilty and stand out on his own recognisance	Arraigned for rescuing himself from James Burke when taken under a civil Bill
William Ryan	Rescue	None	Prisoner was discharged. Prosecutor didn't turn up
John Bryan	Assault	Six months' imprisonment	John Bryan accused of assault with intent to ravish Ellen Clue, a girl of 12. Jury returned verdict of conviction to assault only. 12-month sentence commuted to six (note that this is the City Court)
John Connors	Assault	Four months' imprisonment and to find securities to keep the peace	Found guilty of assault. Information was ordered originally from the petty sessions in April (entry in petty sessions, 5 April)
Stephen Flanigan	Bigamy	Twelve months' imprisonment	Stephen Flanigan indicted for having during the lifetime of his wife Margaret Kelly married Elizabeth Sexton, otherwise Carney
William Russell	Coining	Transportation for seven years	Russell, a private of the 14th dragoons, was indicted for having made 10 penny pieces of counterfeit coin. He was convicted on the evidence of other prisoners and Head Constable Lynn
Patrick Ronan	Coining	Two years with hard labour	Ronan was indicted for having in his possession five counterfeit shillings. Was already on a charge of intending to rob the constabulary after he lost razors he was meant to repair in Carrick. He was under sentence of transportation but the assistant barrister had tried that case without the jurisdiction to do so and it was deemed illegal

Name	Crime	Sentence	Details
Thomas Quirk, Richard Walsh	House-breaking	Twelve months' imprisonment	Walsh and Quirk broke into the storehouse of John Alexander of Greene Street. Head Constable Samuel Lynn matched footprints at the scene to the prisoners. They were arrested by Constable Holmes after he saw their description in *Hue and Cry*. Judge could not sentence them to transportation as it was not a dwelling house they broke into
Bridget Reynolds	Larceny	Six months' imprisonment	John and Bridget Reynolds were indicted for having stolen two pairs of boots; they were found and arrested by Constable O'Hara
Elizabeth Hearne	Larceny	Transportation for seven years	Hearne was indicted for having stolen nine yards of calico, twelve of cashmere, a shawl and other articles from the shop of William Banks of High Street. She had kept the tickets for the articles stolen on her person having pawned the stolen goods
John Reynolds	Larceny	Six months' imprisonment	John and Bridget Reynolds were indicted for having stolen two pairs of boots. They were found and arrested by Constable O'Hara
Margaret Phelan	Larceny	Six months' imprisonment	Phelan was indicted for stealing nine yards of cloth, property of JB Nowlan. Sub-Constable David Nicholson found the cloth in her house
Bridget Flynn	Larceny	Nine months' imprisonment	Flynn was indicted for stealing a coat, a gown and a handkerchief, property of Anastasia Walsh. Commuted from seven years transportation
Thomas Kerevan	Larceny	Four months' imprisonment	Kerevan was indicted for stealing 3 stone of potatoes, property of Godfrey Greene, valued at 6d.
Anne McLoughlin	Larceny	Four months' imprisonment	McLoughlin was charged with having stolen two gowns, property of Michael Byrne. Obtained a good character reference and was recommended to mercy

Name	Crime	Sentence	Details
Mary Connell	Larceny	Acquitted	Connell was indicted for stealing an apron, the property of Ellen Hackett; acquitted due to lack of evidence; noted as being a member of a most notorious family of thieves
Mary Davy	Larceny	Five months' imprisonment	Davy was indicted for having stolen a cloak, property of Ellen Shortall
Mary Hayes	Larceny	Acquitted	Hayes was indicted for stealing a cloak and other property belonging to John Fleming. Charges mainly based on evidence of Bridget Brennan, whom jury appeared not to believe
Mary Kerevan, Catherine Ryan	Receiving stolen goods	Acquitted	Kerevan and Ryan were indicted for having in their possession 2 jugs valued at 6*d.* each. No identification of the prisoners was given. They were acquitted
Denis Bergin	Rescue	Acquitted	Bergin was charged with rescuing a table and other furniture from John Kenehan who had seized them under a civil decree

PETTY SESSIONS SENTENCES, COMPILED FROM THE CASES REPORTED IN THE
KILKENNY JOURNAL AND *KILKENNY MODERATOR*, JANUARY TO DECEMBER 1845

Name	Crime	Sentence	Details
Kyran Cody	Abandoning his children	Warrant issued for his arrest, to be given two weeks' hard labour on his return and to take back and support his children	Patrick Talbot's son-in-law left his 3 children in his care and abandoned them; he admitted them to the workhouse on condition that informations on abandonment be sworn
Thomas Delany	Assault	Fine of 2s. 6d. or imprisonment for 48 hours	Sub-Constable Shaw arrested Delany on the parade for being drunk. He was assaulted on making the arrest
Edmund Prendergast	Assault	Committed to bail and to keep the peace	Admitted to bail for assault on Kinna to sum of £20 and 2 sureties of £10 each
Various	Assault	Unknown, eight persons bound to the peace	Large numbers of assault and threatening language mostly of a trivial nature. Eight persons bound to the peace
John Walshe, James Walshe	Assault	Committed to bail and to keep the peace	Admitted to bail for assault on Kinna to sum of £20 and 2 sureties of £10 each
John Connors	Assault	Informations were ordered by the magistrates. Case carried forward to quarter sessions. Subsequently published in *Kilkenny Moderator*, 30 July	John Connors accused by Ann Curry and Winifred Dalton of coming into Ann Curry's house and attempting to forcibly remove a deserted child left in Winifred's care. Connors stated that the child was his and that he was assaulted by Dalton first
Susan Comerford	Assault	5s. fine and one week's imprisonment	Prosecuted by Bridget Murphy for assault. Comerford bought lace off Murphy but refused to pay and threatened to stick her with a knife: 'was hearty on one occasion and drunk on another'
Andrew Kenna	Assault	Bound to the peace, fined 5s. or imprisoned for four days	John G.A. Prim complained that Kenna followed him on the Cork road and used abusive language and threw stones at him; latter part of sentence remitted at request of complainant

Name	Crime	Sentence	Details
Thomas Fitzgerald	Assault	Fined 1s. or imprisonment for 24 hours	Admitted the impropriety of his conduct and stated his regret
Anastasia Delany	Assault	Informations taken to send to quarter sessions	Anastasia Delany proven to have beaten Anastasia Burke upon the head with a hammer
John McDonald (Constable)	Assault	£2 fine or one month's imprisonment	Sub-Constable McDonald summoned for assaulting Thomas Millea, striking him on the head with his baton. Constable John O'Hara and Henry Logan were also included in the complaint
James Sheehan	Assault	Fine of £1 or imprisonment for one week with hard labour	Charged with having been drunk and riotous in the public streets, resisting arrest and assaulting Constable Rice, Acting Constable Roche and Sub-Constable Anderson. He also bit Roche on the leg. Court decided against sending him to quarter sessions where Mr O'Gorman would not have been so lenient
James Rawlins	Assault	Fine of £1 or imprisonment for a fortnight	James Smee, a turnkey in the city prison, charged Rawlins with assault. He was brought in drunk on Saturday evening. Rawlins was told he could attend mass on Sunday morning and got violent, stating he was not a Catholic and that the turnkey tried to compel him to attend the service
John Dwyer	Assault	5s. fine or a week's imprisonment in default of payment	Charged with assault on a soldier while very drunk
Not Given	Ballad singing	Ordered to return to Bagenalstown	Collected a crowd and impeded a public passage by singing ballads. She had pawned her cloak and needed 1s. to claim it back, the judge gave her 1s.

Name	Crime	Sentence	Details
Martin Dunn	Breach of the Excise laws	Fined £50 but an appeal to the Excise board was not objected to	Charged by Thomas Heathcote, supervisor of Excise, with having spirits on his premises with no permit. Head Constable Lynn found a keg with 5 gallons of 20% proof spirits under his counter
Joseph McDonnell	Breach of the Spirit Licence Act	Fine of 10s. and costs	Head Constable Lynn found that spirits were being sold at a prohibited hour
Thomas Croak	Breach of the Spirit Licence Act	Fine of 10s. minimum allowed by law	Constable David Baird charged Croak with permitting persons to drink in his public house at prohibited hours. Head Constable confirmed that it was his first offence
Margaret Smith	Child abandonment	Bench refused to receive information	Bench refused to receive information as she had sworn information against a party who had abandoned the baby in her house previously
Michael Ryan	Child abandonment	One week's confinement	Ryan was working for a mason, Michael Holmes, and absconded to Dublin leaving his child. Informations were sworn against him and he was arrested in Dublin and returned to Kilkenny
William Finucane Junior, William Finucane Senior, Mahon	Conspiracy to take a life	Case did not warrant the taking of informations or issuing of warrants	The two Finucanes and Mahon used threatening and abusive language to Capt. Rogers of the Pensioners after pensions were stopped. A charge of conspiracy to murder was brought forward but dismissed
John Dunn	Criminal damage	Fine of 6d. or imprisonment for twelve hours	John Magrath charged Dunn with entering his shop and extinguishing his gas light with a piece of paper containing gunpowder. Dunn stated he didn't know the paper had gunpowder in it. He got the paper off another boy named Comerford to light a pipe

Name	Crime	Sentence	Details
Michael O'Brien	Criminal damage	£5 fine or two months' imprisonment; sentence then deferred; he was fined 1*d*. or one hour's imprisonment	Michael Phelan, the master of the workhouse, complained that an inmate Michael O'Brien had broken windows after he was put out of the workhouse being able to work. O'Brien claimed that he had acted in order to subsist. After agreeing to pay the damages, and after the case being commented on in the papers, he was fined one penny
James Comerford	Criminal damage	Fine of 1*s*. or 24 hours' imprisonment	John Magrath charged Dunn with entering his shop and extinguishing his gas light with a piece of paper containing gunpowder. Dunn stated he didn't know the paper had gunpowder in it. He got the paper off Comerford to light a pipe
John Cody	Cruelty to animals	Fine of 5*s*. or a week's imprisonment	Constable John O'Hara summoned Cody for whipping a horse, one thigh of which was broken
James Keogh	Cutting, barking or injuring trees	One week's imprisonment with hard labour	Cutting boughs off a tree on the canal walk
John Smithwick	Cutting or barking trees	One week's imprisonment with hard labour	Cutting boughs off a tree on the canal walk
John Mulhall	Dangerous driving	Fined for negligent driving 2*s*. 6*d*., penalty was remitted by Mr Hamilton	Mulhall was driving a coach from Castlecomer and collided with Mr Hamilton's coach and four on John's Bridge
John Magrath	Detaining in his possession an ass and car	None	A stranger hired her ass and car and went to Kilkenny and stayed at the defendants inn for seven days and left without paying the bill. Magistrates could not compel the defendant to give up the property without payment of the bill as the plaintiff's son had been drawn in by the swindler. Description of swindler was placed in *Hue and Cry*

Name	Crime	Sentence	Details
Anne Murphy	Disorderly conduct	5s. fine or a week's imprisonment	Anne Murphy, a celebrated flagrante on the pave, fined for trespass on the grounds of Edmond Mulhallen. Two men in her company also fined
John Parsons	Drunkenness	Fine of 2s. 6d. or 24 hours' imprisonment	Head Constable Lynn complained that Parsons was drunk and disorderly in the streets and obstructed the passage of women
Various	Failure to pay poor rates	Order made to pay rates	Sixteen cases brought before petty sessions court for non-payment of rates. Decrees were granted for unpaid amounts
Various	Failure to pay poor rates	Dismissed	Case was dismissed against all the defendants as separate notices were not served to all the defendants prior to the application for summons
Daniel Kelly	Forgery	Informations ordered; case sent to next quarter sessions	Kelly forged the signatures of Michael Cormack and Pierce Dowling on an I.O.U. for £2
Patrick Murphy, Anthony Murphy	Illegally taking away manure	Fined 1s.	Charged by John Butler with having swept and carried away a quantity of the street manure on Walkin Street. Defendants claimed they only swept away the portion before their door
Dennis Dwyer	Keeping a disorderly house	Dismissed	Constable Baird summoned Dwyer for keeping a disorderly house, that it was constantly filled with people engaged in drunken brawls and gambling, was open at all hours of the night and morning and harboured females of improper character. Case was initially put over to next court day as both defendant and complainant had hired the same attorney who was not aware he had been left a fee by Dwyer, who then made a solemn promise that he amend the ways of his house

Name	Crime	Sentence	Details
Mary Walsh, Catherine Brennan, James Gwynne	Keeping a house of ill fame	Informations were sworn; case adjourned to next quarter sessions	Mary Kealy charged Gwynne, Brennan and Walsh with keeping in Poyntz Lane improper houses and harbouring people of improper character to the public scandal and nuisance
Peggy Grace, Mary Grace, Betty Bryan	Larceny	Summons issued	Heads of cabbage reserved for seed were stolen. A witness was called and named the 3 women. Very serious charge liable to 6 months' imprisonment or £20 fine
James Canning	Malicious injury	Fined 1s. with costs	Gaol Governor Peter Duncan charged Canning with breaking a pane of glass while confined for drunkenness
Various	Non-payment of rates	Case dismissed	22 cases of non-payment of rates were brought forward by Mr Brennan, the city poor rate collector. Case dismissed as there was a mistake on the summons form, people were directed to appear 'one o clock at noon'
Patrick Farrel	Not releasing Thomas Power from his indentures	Ordered to release Power from his indentures	Neglected Power's indenture, Power advised to sue for his indenture fee of £3
Michael Dunphy	Obstructing a public pathway	Ordered to pay the cost of the summons	Dunphy was summoned by Sub-Constable Kelly for obstructing public passage on John Street by having upon it a quantity of coal and culm
Patrick Fitzgerald	Plaintiff was bitten by a dog	Dismissed	John Egan complained that, as he passed Fitzgerald's house, he was bitten by a dog. Fitzgerald stated that the dog wasn't his. He had given it to a man named Meighan, 12 months previously, to mind an orchard
John Blanchfield	Possession of an unregistered firearm	Fined 2s. 6d., gun to remain with police until registered	Constable John Barns charged John Blanchfield with having on 20 March an unregistered firearm

Name	Crime	Sentence	Details
Bridget Walsh	Refusing to give evidence	Case put off to the next court day	Sub-Constable Henry Logan complained that Walsh refused to give evidence in a case of larceny. She was allowed to consider the matter until the next court day
Michael Magrath	Refusing to take soldiers on billet	Ordered to pay 6d. and costs	Sergeant Michael Wafer of the 10th regiment was recruiting and requested that Magrath billet two recruits. Magrath said he had no room and offered to put them up in a lodging house. The sergeant refused this offer, the cost of billeting the soldiers falls to the publican in these cases
Patrick Magrath	Rescue	Informations granted to bring the case to quarter sessions (early 1846)	Prosecution stated that they had no authority as to whether or not the mayor had acted legally in issuing the warrant. They had only to ascertain whether there was a case for reference to the Barristers' Court
Anne Downes, Margaret Magrath, Catherine Murphy	Stealing potatoes	One month's imprisonment, with every alternate day at hard labour	Convicted of stealing potatoes, the property of Richard Magrath
Martin Maddigan	Summoned for not paying poor rates	Warrant was ordered for amount ordered	Thomas Brennan summoned Maddigan for the sum of £2 1s. 9d., amount of rates due from several tenants as lessor; Maddigan claimed the rates were incorrect
Unknown	Summoned for not paying poor rates	Dismissed on a technicality	Case dismissed on the ground of infamiliarity in the drawing and serving of the notices directed
Mary Corcoran, Judith Phelan	Threatening language	Bound to keep the peace for three years	Using threatening language to Johanna Corcoran
Joseph Fennelly, Joseph Walsh	Trespass	Payment of costs to the court	Fennelly and Walsh were charged by Patrick Butler, caretaker to the marquis, with trespass upon and breaking trees and committing other injuries on the grounds of Kilkenny Castle

Name	Crime	Sentence	Details
John Butler	Trespass	Case dismissed	Charged with committing trespass on his lands
Patrick Guilfoile	Using abusive language	Bound to keep the peace	Summoned by a pensioner, William Finegan, for using language calculated to excite him to breach the peace
Bridget Meara, Mary Walsh, John Walsh	Using threatening and abusive language	Bound to the peace	Bridget Meara complained of John and Mary Walsh using violent and abusive language; John Walsh was found innocent; it was an argument between the two women. Mr Scott lamented that the ancient law of the ducking stool for the punishment of scolds was not revived as fully two-thirds of cases which came into the court were the results of squabbles between viragos
James Cantwell	Using violent and abusive language	Dismissed	Thomas Howard summoned James Cantwell for using violent and abusive language. The case was dismissed as a dispute between tradesmen

Notes

CRF   Convict Reference Files, National Archives, Dublin
CSORP   Chief Secretary's Office Registered Papers, National Archives, Dublin
HC   House of Commons
KCA   Kilkenny Corporation Archive
KCL   Kilkenny County Library
NAI   National Archives of Ireland
NLI   National Library of Ireland

INTRODUCTION

1 Desmond McCabe, 'Law conflict and social order: Mayo 1820–1845' (PhD, University College Dublin, 1991); R.J. McMahon, 'The courts of petty sessions and the law in pre-Famine Galway' (MA thesis, University College Galway, 1999); Imelda Moloney, 'Kilmoganny Petty Sessions' (BA thesis, Maynooth University, 2011).

2 NLI, MS 14,902 Westport Petty Sessions Book.

3 NAI, CSORP/1845/G4650.

4 *Report of the commissioners appointed to take the census of Ireland, for the year 1841*, HC 1843 [504] xxiv, pp 159–64.

5 *First report of commissioners for inquiring into the condition of the poorer classes in Ireland* HC 1835 (369) xxxii, Pt i, 1, xxxii Pt ii, 1 pp 881–3.

6 *Poor inquiry (Ireland). Appendix (C.)— Parts I. and II. Part I. Reports on the state of the poor, and on the charitable institutions in some of the principal towns; with supplement containing answers to queries*, HC 1836 [35] [36] [37] [38] [39] [40] [41] [42] xxx, 35, 221, xxxi,1, xxxii,1, xxxiii,1, xxxiv,1, 427, 643, 657.

7 *Evidence taken before Her Majesty's commissioners of inquiry into the state of the law and practice in respect to the occupation of land in Ireland. Part iii*, HC 1845 [657], xxi, 1 pp 362–7, 382–3. *Appendix to minutes of evidence taken before Her Majesty's commissioners of inquiry into the state of the law and practice in respect to the occupation*

of land in Ireland. Part iv, HC 1845 [672] [673], xxii, 1, 225.

8 *Evidence taken before Her Majesty's commissioners of inquiry into the state of the law and practice in respect to the occupation of land in Ireland. Part iii*, HC 1845 [657], xxi, 1 pp 382, 383.

9 *Report from the select committee of the House of Lords, appointed to enquire into the state of Ireland in respect of crime, and to report thereon to the House; with the minutes of evidence taken before the committee, and an appendix and index. Part i. Report,—and evidence, 22 April to 16 May 1839*, HC 1839 (486) xi,1, xii,1, also *Part iii. Report, and evidence, 12 June to 19 July 1839*, HC 1839 (486).

10 *State of Ireland, Part iii*, pp 47–54.

11 Ibid., *Part i*, pp 541–81.

12 Ibid., *Part i*, p. 543.

13 Ibid., pp 852–5, *State of Ireland, Part iii*, pp 427, 428.

14 NAI, CSORP, 1845, G4650.

15 KCA, Kilkenny Corporation minute book, No. 10, 1843 to 1851, pp 153–280.

16 Ibid., pp 212–13.

17 Ibid., p. 214.

18 KCL, Kilkenny board of guardians' minute books, 1845, BG101A,

19 Ibid., p. 238 and *Kilkenny Journal*, 8 Jan. 1845.

20 KCL, Kilkenny board of guardians' minute books, 1845, BG101A, pp 268, 269, 310, 323, 359.

21 Ibid., p. 495.

22 *Committals (Ireland). Returns from the clerks of the crown and clerks of the peace of the*

several counties, &c. in Ireland, of the number of persons committed to the different gaols thereof for trial, in the year 1845, HC 1846 (46), xxxv, 1, p. 38.

23 *Prisons of Ireland. Twenty-fourth report of the inspectors-general on the general state of the prisons in Ireland with Appendices 1845; with appendices*, HC 1846 [697], xx, 257, pp 332, 333.

24 *Prisons of Ireland. Twentieth report of the inspectors-general on the general state of the prisons in Ireland with appendices 1842: with appendices*, HC 1843 [462], xxvii, 83, stated that it had three day rooms while the report of 1846, *Prisons of Ireland, twenty first report of the inspectors-general on the general state of the prisons in Ireland with appendices, 1847*, HC 1847–48 [952], xxxiv, 253, pp 346–7, stated that it had eight cells.

25 *Prisons of Ireland. Twenty-fourth report of the inspectors-general on the general state of the prisons in Ireland with appendices*, HC 1843, [462] xxvii, 83, p. 156.

26 Griffin, p. 30.

27 NAI, CRF, 1845, C40; CRF, 1845, D7; CRF, 1845, D10; CRF, 1845, D3; CRF, 1845, K27.

I. KILKENNY IN 1845

1 *Report of the commissioners appointed to take the census of Ireland, for the year 1841*, HC 1843 [504] xxxiv, 1.

2 *Municipal corporation boundaries (Ireland). Copy of instructions given by his excellency the lord lieutenant of Ireland, with reference to the boundaries and division into wards of the several cities, boroughs and towns corporate in Ireland; Reports and plans*. HC 1837 (301) xxix, 3, pp 196–9.

3 *Municipal corporations (Ireland). A bill for the regulation of municipal corporations in Ireland*. HC 1840 (97) i, 641, pp 641, 655 also *Municipal districts regulation. (Ireland.) A bill to annex certain parts of certain counties of cities to adjoining counties for fiscal purposes, and for certain purposes of civil and criminal jurisdiction*, HC 1840 (529) i, 799, pp 799–800; also KCL, grand jury minute books, Kilkenny city, Spring 1845.

4 *Census of Ireland, 1841*.

5 Oliver Mac Donagh, 'The economy and society, 1830–1845' in W.E. Vaughan (ed.), *A new history of Ireland; v, Ireland*

under the Union, 1801–1870 (Oxford, 2010), pp 218–41; also T.W. Freeman, 'Land and people, c.1841' in Vaughan (ed.), *New history of Ireland, v*, pp 242–65.

6 Cormac Ó Grada, 'Poverty population and agriculture, 1801–1845' in Vaughan (ed.), *New history of Ireland, v*, p. 115.

7 *First report of commissioners for inquiring into the condition of the poorer classes in Ireland, Supplement to Appendix D*, HC 1836 [36] xxxii I p. 182.

8 KCL, Kilkenny board of guardians' minute books, 1845, BG101A, pp 268, 269, 310, 323, 359.

9 KCL, Kilkenny board of guardians' minute books, 1845, BG101A, pp 268, 269.

10 Ibid., pp 494, 495.

11 Ibid., pp 310, 323, 324, 359.

12 KCL, Kilkenny board of guardians' minute books, 1845, BG101A, p. 233.

13 Ibid., pp 226–7, 510, 511, 535, 566, 576.

14 Robert Cane, *Some practical remarks on cholera with an appendix containing sanatory hints for Kilkenny* (Kilkenny, 1849), pp 23–57.

15 Based on *Report of the commissioners appointed to take the census of Ireland, for the year 1841*, HC 1843 [504], xxiv, pp 156–61, hereafter *Census of Ireland, 1841*.

16 Cane, *Practical remarks*, p 29.

17 Ibid., pp 23–57.

18 *Census of Ireland, 1841*, p. 14.

19 Cane, *Practical remarks*, pp 23–4.

20 MacDonagh, 'The economy and society, 1830–1845', pp 218–41.

21 Robert Cane, *Practical remarks*, pp 34–6.

22 *First report of commissioners for inquiring into the condition of the poorer classes in Ireland* HC 1835 (369) xxii. Appendix A, p. 882 (hereafter *Poor Law Report*).

23 *Poor Law Report* (369), HC xxxii Pt I, 1, pp 882–3.

24 *Poor Law Report*, Supplement to Appendix D, p 182.

25 *Kilkenny Moderator*, 8 Jan. 1845.

26 *Poor Law Report*, Supplement to Appendix E, p. 178.

27 Ibid., p. 178.

28 *Evidence taken before Her Majesty's commissioners of inquiry into the state of the law and practice in respect to the occupation of land in Ireland. Part iii*, HC 1845 [657], xxi, 1, pp 382–3.

29 *Kilkenny Moderator*, 28 May 1845.
30 *Devon commission*, Part iii, p 383.
31 Ibid., p 367.
32 *Kilkenny Moderator*, 26 Feb. 1845.
33 Cane, *Practical remarks*, pp 24–5.
34 *Kilkenny Journal*, 5 July 1845.
35 *Kilkenny Moderator*, 15 Jan. 1845.

2. CRIME AND SENTENCING IN 1845

1 R.B. McDowell, 'The Irish courts of law, 1801–1914', *Irish Historical Studies*, 10:40 (Sept. 1957), 363–91.
2 Richard Nun and John Edward Walsh, *Justices of the peace in Ireland, and of constables as connected therewith, with an appendix of statutes and forms* (Dublin, 1841) and Edmond Hayes, *Crimes and punishments; or; an analytical digest of the criminal statute law of Ireland* (Dublin, 1837).
3 Geo IV, c 67, 7 & 8 George IV, 1827.
4 Desmond McCabe, 'Magistrates, peasants and the petty sessions courts: Mayo, 1823–50', *Cathair na Mart*, 5:1 (1985), 45–53.
5 McCabe, 'Magistrates, peasants and the petty sessions courts'; also Marilyn Silverman, 'Custom, courts and class formation: constructing the hegemonic process through the petty sessions of a southeastern Irish parish, 1828–1884', *American Ethnologist*, 27:2 (May 2000), 400–30.
6 *A bill for the better administration of justice at the holding of petty sessions by justices of the peace in Ireland*, HC 1826 (297), ii, 497 and *Petty sessions. (Ireland.) A bill to amend an act passed in the seventh and eighth years of the reign of His Majesty King George the Fourth, for the better administration of justice at the holding of petty sessions by justices of the peace in Ireland*, HC 1836 (243), iv, 527.
7 Silverman, 'Custom, courts and class formation', p. 406.
8 *Petty sessions (Ireland). Return of the petty sessions held in Ireland during 1842*, HC 1843 (543) li, pp 61–2.
9 V.T.H. Delany, *The administration of justice in Ireland* (Dublin, 1980), pp 26–8.
10 Ibid.
11 *Kilkenny Moderator* and *Kilkenny Journal*, Jan. to Dec. 1845.
12 Delany, *The administration of justice in Ireland* pp 26–7.

13 *Kilkenny Moderator* and *Kilkenny Journal*, Jan. to Dec. 1845.
14 Ned McHugh, 'Crime and punishment: Drogheda, 1830–1844: an analysis of returns of committals for trial', *Journal of the County Louth Historical and Archaeological Society*, 25:2 (2002), 152–4, 157; *Kilkenny Moderator, Kilkenny Journal*, Jan. to Dec. 1845
15 NAI, CSORP, G4648, 1845, this is a letter from the crown solicitor on the Leinster circuit, William Kemmis, to the chief secretary acknowledging receipt of an instruction to distinguish offences relating to land, Whiteboy offences and robbery of arms to those of a different character. This letter is appended to G4650 and is the first letter in this file.
16 NAI, CSORP, G4650, 1845. This is a list of all offences tried at the assizes on all the circuits in 1845.
17 Desmond McCabe, 'That part that laws or kings can cause or cure: crown prosecution and jury trial at Longford Assizes, 1830–45' in Raymond Gillespie and Gerard Moran (eds), *Longford: essays in county history* (Dublin, 1991) pp 153–72.
18 McHugh, 'Crime and punishment', pp 152–7.
19 *Kilkenny Moderator*, 23 Apr. 1845.
20 *First report of the commissioners appointed to inquire into the municipal corporations in Ireland*, HC 1835 [23–8], xxvii, 1, 51, 79, 199, p. 84.
21 *Kilkenny Moderator*, 12 Mar. 1845, *Kilkenny Journal*, 23 July 1845.
22 Tables 4 and 5 are compiled from the grand jury minute books for the city assizes for 1845, KCL, grand jury minute books, Kilkenny city, spring 1845, winter 1845.
23 KCA, Kilkenny Corporation minute book, No. 10, 1843 to 1851, p. 214.

3. CRIME AND SENTENCING IN KILKENNY CITY IN 1845

1 *Kilkenny Moderator*, 29 Nov. 1845.
2 McCabe, 'Law conflict and social order, Mayo, 1820–1845', and McMahon, 'The courts of petty sessions and the law in pre-Famine Galway'.
3 *Kilkenny Moderator*, 29 May, 10 Dec. 1845.

4   *Kilkenny Moderator*, 8 Jan., 6 Aug., 29 Nov. 1845.

5   Ireland, *tables showing the number of criminal offenders committed for trial or bailed for appearance at the assizes and sessions in each county, in the year 1845, and the result of the proceedings. Chief Secretary's Office, Dublin Castle, March, 1846*, HC 1846, [696], xxxv, 81, p. 9.

6   *Kilkenny Moderator*, 29 May 1845.

7   Ibid., 6 Aug. 1845.

8   *Kilkenny Moderator*, 8 Jan., 5 Apr., 29 May, 15 Oct., 12 Nov., 10 Dec. 1845 and *Kilkenny Journal*, 5 Apr. and 12 Nov. 1845.

9   *Kilkenny Moderator*, 5 Apr. 1845 and 15 Oct. 1845.

10 Ibid., 21 Mar. 1840.

11 Ibid., 3 Sept. 1845.

12 Ibid., 10 Dec. 1845.

13 Ibid., 6 Aug. 1845.

14 Ibid., 8 Jan. and 15 Oct. 1845.

15 Ibid., 13 Aug. 1845.

16 Ibid., 16 Aug. 1845.

17 Ibid., 8 Jan. 1845.

18 *Kilkenny Journal*, 12 Nov. 1845.

19 *Kilkenny Moderator*, 29 May 1845.

20 Ibid., 26 July 1845, 30 July 1845

21 Ibid., 26, 30 July 1845.

22 *State of Ireland*, Part iii, pp 428–30.

23 *Kilkenny Journal*, 12 Feb. 1845.

24 *Committals (Ireland). Returns of the number of persons committed to the different gaols thereof for trial, in the year 1845*, HC 1846 (46), xxxv, 1, p. 38 and Ireland, *tables showing the number of criminal offenders committed for trial or bailed for appearance at the assizes and sessions in each county, in the year 1845, and the result of the proceedings. Chief Secretary's Office, Dublin Castle, March, 1846*, HC 1846 [696], xxxv, 81, p. 127; these are two examples of these papers.

25 NAI, CSORP, G4650, 1845.

26 McHugh, 'Crime and punishment', p. 158.

27 *Committals (Ireland), 1845*, HC 1846 (46) xxxv, 1.

28 Compiled from the various *Tables showing the number of criminal offenders committed for trial or bailed* etc. for the years 1845 to 1850.

29 *Kilkenny Journal*, 15 Jan. 1845.

30 *Kilkenny Moderator*, 30 July 1845.

31 Ibid., 30 July 1845.

32 *Kilkenny Journal*, 29 Oct. 1845.

33 Ibid., 5 Nov. 1845 and *Kilkenny Moderator*, 1 Nov. 1845.

34 *Kilkenny Moderator*, 30 July 1845.

35 Ibid., 5 Apr. 1845.

36 Ibid., 1 Nov. 1845.

37 NAI, Transportation Register 6, p. 297 and NAI, Convict Reference Files, 1845, 48 was the file that was unavailable. Extracts from the transportation registers are available online at the following address, the complete list is also available online: http://findingaids.nationalarchives.ie/index.php?category=18&advanced=true&subcategory=147 accessed 1 Jan. 2012.

38 *Kilkenny Moderator*, 30 July 1845 and ibid., 5 Apr. 1845.

39 Ibid., 30 July 1845.

40 The four instances of rescue were reported as follows: *Kilkenny Moderator*, 30 July 1845, 29 Oct. 1845, 5 Nov. 1845 and 10 Dec. 1845.

41 *Kilkenny Journal*, 12 Apr., 20 Aug. 1845 and *Kilkenny Moderator*, 30 July, 9, 13, 20, Aug. 1845.

42 NAI, CRF 1845, k27 and *Kilkenny Moderator*, 5 Apr. 1845.

CONCLUSION

1   Ireland, *tables showing the number of criminal offenders committed for trial or bailed for appearance at the assizes and sessions in each county, in the year 1845*, p. 9.

2   Michel Foucault, *Discipline and punish: the birth of the prison* (New York, 1995), p. 232.

3   Foucault, *Discipline and punish*, p. 232.

4   *Kilkenny Moderator*, 15 Jan. 1845.